SH*TS
— and —
GIGGLES

THE ULTIMATE
BATHROOM JOKE BOOK

SH*TS

— and —

GIGGLES

THE ULTIMATE
BATHROOM JOKE BOOK

KATIE ADAMS

Castle Point Books
NEW YORK

www.stmartins.com
www.castlepointbooks.com

The Castle Point Books trademark is owned by Castle Point Publications, LLC.
Castle Point books are published and distributed by St. Martin's Press.

Illustrations used under license from Shutterstock.com

ISBN 978-1-250-16410-0 (trade paperback)

Our books may be purchased in bulk for promotional, educational, or business
use. Please contact your local bookseller or the Macmillan Corporate and
Premium Sales Department at 1-800-221-7945, extension 5442,
or by e-mail at MacmillanSpecialMarkets@macmillan.com.

First Edition: April 2018

10 9 8 7 6 5 4 3 2 1

Contents

4 Love and Other Silly Things 49

5 NNNEEERRRDDDSSS!!!! 81

1

STUFF YOU SHOULDN'T EVER SAY, TELL, HEAR, OR THINK

SUPER INAPPROPRIATE JOKES THAT YOU SHOULD NEVER TELL IN POLITE COMPANY

Best to just keep these to yourself.

What should you do if you come across an old woman crossing the street?
Apologize and wipe it off.

What is the best way to ensure a guy will remember the color of your eyes?
Be an A cup.

How is parenting like toilet paper?
You're either on a roll, or dealing with a bunch of shit.

What's the difference between a rabbi and a priest?
One cuts 'em, the other sucks 'em.

Why did the prostitute ask for a loan?
She needed a bit of help until she got off her feet again.

Why did the man cry when he masturbated?
He was a tearjerker.

What type of bird gives the best blow jobs?
A swallow.

What did the off-duty prostitute say to the man in the car?
"Beat it, I'm off the clock."

What did the man's poop smell like?
Shit.

ALL THE DIFFERENT WAYS YOU CAN CALL BULLSHIT

Let's face it: Our world is full of more bullshit now than ever before. Which is to say you should have more than one word for it in your arsenal the next time you need to call it out.

Baboonery	Drivel	Posh posh
Balderdash	Flapdoodle	Rhubarb
Balls	Flim-flam	Rubbish
Ballyhoo	Gobble-gabble	Shit sandwich
Batshit	Hocus-pocus	Shite
Bird turd	Hogwash	Trumpery
Blarney	Horse feathers	Twaddle
Blather	Horse shit	Weasel words
Bollocks	Irish bull	Yakety-yak
Bull farts	Jibber jabber	
Bunk bull	Load	
Cock and bull	Macaroni	
Codswallop	Malarkey	
Cowyard confetti	Mumble jumbo	
Crap	Nitshit	
Crapspackle	Phooey	
Crock	Pish and tush	
Donkey dust	Poppycock	

NOT-SO-SEXY
FORTUNES

We've all played that game at a Chinese restaurant where you add "in bed" to the end of your fortune cookie fortune. Here are some actual fortunes that will make your game delightfully awkward.

> You will get a visit from an unexpected relative.

> You will have many children.

> A friend asks only for your time, not your money.

> Don't confuse recklessness with confidence.

> A person is never too old or too young to learn.

> Never hesitate to tackle the most difficult problems.

> It's amazing how much good you can do if you don't care who gets the credit.

> A stranger is just a friend you haven't met.

> You can make your own happiness.

> There is no greater pleasure than seeing your loved ones prosper.

What's Black and White and Read All Over?

The original answer is "newspaper," but those don't exist anymore. Nor is it a very exciting answer. So here are some better ones that play Jedi mind tricks with that nice little homophone.

What's black and white and red all over?
An embarrassed skunk.

....

What's black and white and red all over?
A zebra in a red sweatsuit.

....

What's black and white and red all over?
A sunburned penguin.

....

What's black and white and red all over?
Oreos dipped in strawberry jam.

....

What's black and white and red all over?
A referee who spilled cherry Kool-Aid on himself.

....

What's black and white and red all over?
Two nuns in a chainsaw fight.

....

What's black and white and red all over?
A panda that spilled some paint.

....

What's black and white and red all over?
A penguin in a blender.

....

What's black and white and red all over?
A panda in a red dress.

....

What's black and white and red all over?
A zebra with a rash.

....

What's black and white and red all over?
A skunk dipped in ketchup.

....

What's black and white and red all over?
A polar bear eating a penguin.

....

What's black and white and red all over?
A newspaper with a printing error.

....

What's black and white and red all over?
A poorly colorized black-and-white movie.

....

What's black and white and red all over?
The devil in a tuxedo.

....

What's black and white and red all over?
A zebra who is a Communist.

....

MORE EUPHEMISMS FOR "FART" AND "FARTING" THAN YOU WILL EVER NEED

Not to blow a bunch of hot air, but this page stinks.

- A panty burp
- Sphincter whistle
- Pop tart
- Fanny beep
- Anal exhale
- Anal exaltation
- Cornhole clap
- Hot wind
- Crack splitter
- Butt yodel
- Cheek squeak
- Taint tickler
- Taint ripper
- Seam breaker
- Grundle rumbler
- Trouser trumpet
- Pants music
- Anus applause

- Benchwarmer
- Rectal turbulence
- Blowing the sparkplugs
- Hummerrhoids
- Cutting muffins
- Going colon bowlin'
- Answering the call of the wild burrito
- Blasting the chair
- Bending a valve
- Testing the wind tunnel Rattler
- Roar from the rear
- Wootsy
- The one-cheek sneak
- Turning on the free Jacuzzi
- Blowing a gasket
- A power puff
- Playing the O-ring oboe

Firing a stink torpedo

Saluting your shorts

Sounding the sphincter siren

Some thunder from
down under

Blowing the big brown horn

Starting the engine

Backend blowout

Cutting the cheese

Launching an air attack

Blast of the ol' butt tuba

Belching clown

Anal retreat

Crunchy frog

Baking brownies

Cornhole tremor

Letting the voice
of the toothless one
be heard

Barn burner

One-man salute

Deer snort

Fanny-tosis

Fire in the hole

Anal evacuation

Booty bomb

Floorboard lift

Floating a biscuit

Drive-by

A message from the
Department of the Interior

Spraying poo-fume

A ringo

A prison break

A scented scream

A silent depth charge

The roaring of the
underpants lion

Mudslapper

Flutterblast

Brown-body radiation

Fartrogen dioxide

Putt-putts

A one-gun salute

A flabbergaster

Gastronomical repercussion

Room clearer

THE ULTIMATE BATHROOM PLAYLIST

Music to take a poop to.

"Make 'Em Say Uhh!" Master P

"Release the Beast," Breakwater

"Help!" The Beatles

"U Can't Touch This," M.C. Hammer

"Chocolate Town," Ween

"The Waiting Is the Hardest Part," Tom Petty and the Heartbreakers

"That Smell," Lynyrd Skynyrd

"Thick as a Brick," Jethro Tull

"Taking Care of Business," Bachman-Turner Overdrive

"Push It," Salt-N-Pepa

"Whip It," Devo

"Da Doo Ron Ron," The Ronettes

"Drop It Like It's Hot," Snoop Dogg ft. Pharrell

"Chocolate Rain," Tay Zonday

"Under Pressure," Queen and David Bowie

"In the Air Tonight," Phil Collins

"Big Log," Robert Plant

HELEN KELLER
JOKES

Keller is an inspiration and a true hero, earning a doctorate, writing books, and lecturing around the world despite being both blind and deaf. For this she deserves our admiration, respect. . . and a page of crass jokes.

How did Helen Keller meet her husband?
She got set up on a blind date.

Have you heard about the Helen Keller Alphabet?
It's just like the regular alphabet, except that there's no C.

Why was Helen Keller late for work?
She got arrested for drunk driving.

What's Helen Keller's favorite color?
Black.

What's Helen Keller's other favorite color?
Corduroy.

What's Helen Keller's **other** other favorite color?
Velcro.

Did you hear Helen Keller got in a car accident?
She didn't check her blind spot.

How come Helen Keller can't drive very well?
Because she's a woman.

Why else can't Helen Keller drive very well?
Because she's been dead for 50 years.

Did you know that Helen Keller had psychic abilities?
She really seemed to have a fourth sense.

Helen Keller loved to play tennis.
For her, it was eternal love.

Why couldn't Helen Keller play high school football?
Because she was an adult.

What's the worst present Helen Keller ever received?
A Rubik's Cube.

How did Helen Keller's parents punish her for swearing?
They washed her hands out with soap.

How do you know if Helen Keller has recently brushed her teeth?
The Gleem in her eye.

Helen Keller walked into a bar.
And several other things as well.

Why did Helen Keller like birthday parties?
Because she didn't have to wear a dumb blindfold
before she hit the piñata.

2

SPORTS!

SPORTS TERMS THAT SOUND DIRTY... BUT AREN'T

For those of you who laugh whenever the announcers on TV say, "end zone."

"Loose ball foul"

"Tight end"

"Squeeze play"

"Putt from the rough"

"Backdoor slider"

"Pull the goalie"

"Sticky wicket"

"Rim shot"

"Muffed punt"

"Take it on the chin"

"Take it to the hole"

"Water hazard"

"Penalty stroke"

"Split the uprights"

"Double elimination"

"Double team"

"Pole position"

"Penetrating the backfield"

"Wide receiver"

"Shuttlecock"

"Upper decker"

"High sticking"

"Tearing up the green"

"Mixed doubles"

"High and tight"

"Banging down low"

"In the slot"

"Illegal touching"

More Than Fore Golf Jokes
These jokes are a hole in one! (Sorry.)

Did you hear about the woman who got stung by a bee while golfing?
It was right between the first and second hole.

Why do men love golf?
Because there are 18 holes.

What's the difference between a lost golf ball and a clitoris?
A man will spend hours looking for the golf ball.

Did you hear about the rookie golfer who got
arrested for indecent exposure?
He misunderstood what the ball washer was for.

A golfer tees up at his favorite course, which is next to a river.
He sees a couple of fishermen and says to his friend,
"Look at those morons fishing in the rain."

Did you hear about the golfer who died on the third hole?
**The rest of his foursome wore themselves out
dragging him around until the 18th hole.**

This one golfer spent so much time in the bunker
that he started getting Hitler's mail.

Golf: For when you're too out of shape for bowling.

Why do golfers always carry an extra pair of pants?
In case they get a hole in one.

What's the name for that huge place full of
hundreds of doctors?
A golf course.

What's the difference between a bad golfer and a bad skydiver?
A bad golfer goes, WHACK! "Damn!"
A bad skydiver goes, "Damn!" WHACK.

A golfer was having such a bad round that he told his caddy,
"I think I'm going to drown myself in the lake."
The caddy replied, "There's no way you could
keep your head down for that long."

How are golf balls like eggs?
They're white, you buy them by the dozen, and you
run out of them after a couple of days.

Why are golf and sex so similar?
You can enjoy them both even if
you're really bad at them.

Do you know why it's called **GOLF**?
All the other four-letter words were taken.

GAMBLING
JOKES

Gambling isn't a sport, but it does involve a high level of
risk and fortunes being made or lost in seconds.

Did you hear about the compulsive gambler's wife who left?

He lost her in a hand of blackjack.

....

What has tiny balls and constantly screws old people?

A bingo cage.

....

Why did the guy quit his job at the casino?

He just couldn't deal.

....

Why is online poker better than playing in a casino?

No man wants another man to watch him have a bad beat.

....

Why don't vampires like to gamble?

The stakes.

What's the difference between a gambler and a politician?

Even politicians tell the truth once in a while.

What did the compulsive gambler say after his wife left him?

"I'd do anything to win her back!"

Who is every gambler's favorite relative?

Their aunty.

What do magazines and gamblers have in common?

In the end, they always fold.

Why should you never play poker in the Serengeti?

Because there are too many cheetahs.

EXTREMELY DISGUSTING WORLD RECORDS

These people make being disgusting seem like an athletic accomplishment.

IN 1999, A MAN ENTERED A HOSPITAL in Saudi Arabia and was diagnosed with an enlarged kidney. Doctors treated an obstruction in urine flow and removed 5.8 gallons of urine from the kidney. That's a world record for worst kidney blockage.

A BRITISH MAN NAMED WILLIAM MCILROY had a condition called Munchausen syndrome, a mental disorder that leads the patient to fake medical problems because they like the attention. Between 1929 and 1979, McIlroy—using 22 fake identities—underwent more than 400 operations at 100 different hospitals. All of them were unnecessary.

IN TERMS OF NECESSARY SURGERIES, that honor goes to Charles Jensen of South Dakota. Between 1954 and 1994, he went through 970 operations to remove facial tumors caused by a genetic disorder.

IN 2010, ARGENTINE DOCTORS REMOVED an 8.7-pound tumor from the uterus of a 54-year-old woman. That one was found to be cancerous. As far as noncancerous tumors go, in 1991 the Stanford University Medical Center needed six hours of surgery to remove a benign 303-pound tumor from a 34-year-old woman.

NORMAL BLOOD GLUCOSE LEVEL: ABOUT 90 TO 100. Anything significantly higher than that means you've probably got diabetes. A seven-year-old boy named Michael Buonocore checked into a Pennsylvania hospital—and was diagnosed with diabetes—when his blood sugar topped out at 26,656.

PASSING A KIDNEY STONE that's the size of a grain of sand is painful. Sandor Sarkadi had his stone surgically removed in 2009: a 2.48-pound, coconut-size kidney stone.

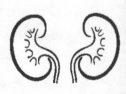

AS FAR AS THE MOST KIDNEY STONES PASSED—all of them tiny, but still—the record belongs to Canadian man Donald Winfield, who spent most of August of 2006 naturally passing 4,504 kidney stones.

HERE'S A TOP PICK! Josh Werner of Connecticut fit a record 2.25 inches of his finger into his nose. (It was his pinky, if you're curious.)

IN 2008, WESLEY WARREN SUFFERED A MEDICAL TRAUMA to the groin, which made his scrotum swell largely and quickly. When he finally got an operation to reduce the swelling, his scrotum weighed 160 pounds.

THEY LIKE THEIR BEANS IN ENGLAND, perhaps none more so than Bernard Clemens of London. He holds the record for the single longest fart: It lasted for a full three minutes.

WEIRD SPORTS INJURIES

PROFESSIONAL ATHLETES: THEY'RE BIG, STRONG, TOUGH, AND EASILY FELLED BY BRAS, SHIRTS, AND BAGPIPES.

Baseball Hall of Famer **Ken Griffey Jr.** once missed some games when his protective cup pinched one of his testicles.

One night, baseball player **Glenallen Hill** was fast asleep and had a nightmare about spiders. He violently fell out of bed and into a glass nightstand. He suffered such severe cuts to his hands and body he wound up on the injured list.

Relief pitcher **John Smoltz** burned several parts of his body when he put on a too-hot, freshly ironed shirt.

· ·

Strikeout king **Nolan Ryan** hurt his hand when he stuck it into an enclosure holding three coyotes. One of the coyotes bit his hand.

· ·

Toronto Maple Leafs goalie **Glenn Healy** needed 40 stitches for a gash on his hand that he got cleaning his bagpipes.

· ·

Pitcher **Adam Eaton** tried to cut the cellophane off a DVD, but his hand slipped and he stabbed himself in the stomach.

· ·

Kevin Mitchell chipped his tooth when he bit into a frozen doughnut that hadn't been properly thawed.

. . . .

NBA star **Lionel Simmons** developed tendonitis in his hands from playing too much Game Boy.

. . . .

Somehow, some way, pro soccer goalie **David Seaman** broke a bone reaching for a remote control in a hotel room.

. . . .

Kim Clijsters couldn't fully participate in the 2011 French Open because she hurt her ankle dancing at a wedding.

. . . .

Roger Craig didn't get his weird injury until he became the manager of the San Francisco Giants. He had a cut-up and bandaged hand—he somehow cut himself while trying to get a woman's bra off in the bedroom.

· ·

NFL kicker **Bill Gramatica** made a 42-yard field goal and jumped up and down in celebration. Then he landed on his foot wrong and tore a muscle in his kicking leg.

· ·

Golfer **Bobby Cruickshank** was in the lead during the final round of the 1934 U.S. Open. The only real trouble he had all day was on the eleventh hole, when he hit a bad shot . . . but then the ball bounced off a rock and landed on the green. Cruickshank was so happy that he threw his club into the air . . . and it fell onto his head. He wound up finishing in third place.

· ·

3

ARE YOU READY TO ROCK, AND ALSO, IF THERE'S TIME, ROLL?

ROCK STAR JOKES

Put down your lighter, stop yelling "Free Bird!" and dig these jokes about rock stars and their devil music.

What was Elvis's last hit?

The bathroom floor.

....

Did you hear that Slash and Madonna had a big fight?

They're no longer on a first-name basis.

....

What has nine arms and sucks?

Def Leppard.

....

Did you hear about the obsessive Beatles collector?

**He has every single one of their records
except for one. He needs HELP!**

....

"Doctor, doctor, you've got to help me. All day long
I want to listen to 'What's New, Pussycat?'"

**"It sounds like you've got Tom Jones syndrome,"
the doctor replied. "But don't worry. . . it's not unusual."**

....

How do you track Will Smith in the snow?

Look for the fresh prints.

....

Did you hear about the accident at the U2 concert?

**Bono fell off the stage. He walked
too close to the Edge.**

....

What's the difference between God and Kanye West?

God doesn't think he's Kanye West.

....

What kind of computer sadly sings "Hello"
whenever you turn it on?

A Dell.

....

Did you hear about the prog-rock band that went fishing?

**They didn't catch anything because
they didn't have any hooks.**

....

Breaking news:

**Sting has been kidnapped.
The Police have no lead.**

....

What's Rob Zombie's real name?

Robert Zombie.

....

Did you hear about the club that couldn't book Eddie Money?

They just didn't have any currency.

....

What did one Grateful Dead fan say to the other
when they ran out of marijuana?

"This band sucks!"

....

What's the difference between a rock musician
and a jazz musician?

**A rock musician plays three chords
in front of thousands,
and a jazz musician plays
thousands of chords
in front of three.**

....

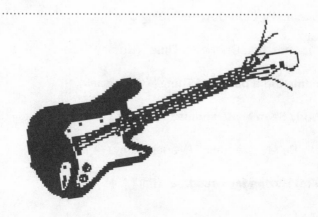

WHAT HAPPENS WHEN YOU REPLACE THE "BABY" IN FAMOUS SONG TITLES WITH "GRANDMA"

For decades, pop music has used the word "baby" as a term of endearment. Frankly, it's weird and a little sick. You know who **really** deserves to have songs written about them? Your wonderful grandmother is who.

"I'm Your Grandma Tonight" (Whitney Houston)

"Grandma Come Back" (Player)

"Grandma's Got a Temper" (The Prodigy)

"Grandma, It's Cold Outside" (Bing Crosby)

"Hit Me Grandma One More Time" (Britney Spears)

"Grandma Did a Bad, Bad Thing" (Chris Isaak)

"Anybody Seen My Grandma?" (Rolling Stones)

"Always Be My Grandma" (Mariah Carey)

"(You're) Having My Grandma" (Paul Anka)

"(You're So Square) Grandma I Don't Care" (Buddy Holly)

"Grandma Hold On" (Eddie Money)

"Grandma, I Need Your Loving" (The Four Tops)

"Grandma, It's You" (The Shirelles)

"Grandma, Come to Me" (Patti Austin and James Ingram)

"Grandma, I Love Your Way" (Peter Frampton)

"Be My Grandma" (The Ronettes)

"Big Bang Grandma" (Stone Temple Pilots)

"Born to Be My Grandma" (Bon Jovi)

"Can't Get Enough of You Grandma" (? and the Mysterians)

"Doing It All for My Grandma" (Huey Lewis and the News)

"Don't Worry Grandma" (The Beach Boys)

"Give It to Me Grandma" (Rick James)

"Ice Ice Grandma" (Vanilla Ice)

"Santa Grandma" (Eartha Kitt)

"Somebody's Grandma" (Jackson Browne)

"Take Good Care of My Grandma" (Bobby Vee)

"Here Comes My Grandma" (Cat Stevens)

"There Goes My Grandma" (The Drifters)

DRUMMER JOKES

There's one guy in every band who's even dumber than the bass player
(and the guitarist, and the singer).

What's the last thing a drummer said to his band?
"Hey guys, let's try one of my songs!"

....

What do you call a drummer who just broke up with his girlfriend?
Homeless.

....

Hear the one about the drummer who graduated from high school?
Me neither.

....

What do you call a guy who hangs out with musicians?
A drummer.

....

What does the average drummer get on an IQ test?
Drool.

....

How can you tell when a stage riser is level?
The drool comes out of both sides of the drummer's mouth.

....

Johnny says to his mom, "I want to be a drummer when I grow up."
Mom says, "But Johnny, you can't do both."

....

Did you hear the one about the guitarist who locked
his keys in the car on the way to a gig?
It took him two hours to get the drummer out.

....

Who wouldn't understand these jokes?
A drummer.

....

MARX OR MARX?

Who said each of the following lines: '80s pop star Richard Marx, or *The Communist Manifesto* author Karl Marx?

a) "From each according to his abilities, to each according to his needs."

b) "We are the children of the night. We won't go down without a fight."

c) "Nothing can have value without being an object of utility."

d) "Hold on to the nights. Hold on to the memory."

e) "Now and forever, I will be your man."

f) "Reason has always existed, but not always in a reasonable form."

g) "Don't you know I won't give up until I'm satisfied?"

h) "Last words are for fools who haven't said enough."

i) "Revolutions are the locomotives of history."

j) "I remember every moment of those endless summer nights."

k) "The meaning of peace is the absence of opposition to socialism."

l) "It don't mean nothing, these games people play."

m) "Should've known better than to fall in love with you."

n) "Freedom is the consciousness of necessity."

Karl: a), c), f), h), i), k), n)

Richard: b), d), e), g), j), l), m)

ANSWERS TO QUESTION SONGS

So many songs have asked questions about the world around them, the nature of love, or the meaning of life. They shouldn't have asked if they didn't expect an answer.

"How Do You Mend a Broken Heart?" (The Bee Gees)
Anesthesia, needle, and thread.

"Where Have All the Flowers Gone?" (Peter, Paul & Mary)
Killed by dog urine.

"Who Let the Dogs Out?" (Baha Men)
Kevin.

"Isn't She Lovely?" (Stevie Wonder)
Not particularly.

"Will You Love Me Tomorrow?" (The Shirelles)
It depends on how tonight goes.

"Who'll Stop the Rain?" (Creedence Clearwater Revival)
Climate change.

"Why Don't We Do It in the Road?" (The Beatles)
Because gravel, and it's rush hour.

"Do You Really Want to Hurt Me?" (Culture Club)
I don't have anything else to do today.

"What's Your Name?" (Lynyrd Skynyrd)
Lynyrd Skynyrd.

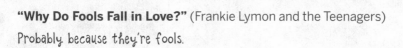

"What's that Smell?" (Lynyrd Skynyrd)
Lynyrd Skynyrd.

"Why Do Fools Fall in Love?" (Frankie Lymon and the Teenagers)
Probably because they're fools.

"Why Can't We Be Friends?" (War)
We voted for different people.

"Do You Know the Way to San Jose?" (Dionne Warwick)
We'll give you directions if you buy something.

"What Is Life?" (George Harrison)
About 80 years.

"Do You Want to Know a Secret?" (The Beatles)
Not really.

"How Will I Know?" (Whitney Houston)
A Google Alert.

"Do You Know the Muffin Man?"
Met him once. He was delicious.

4

LOVE
AND OTHER
SILLY
THINGS

Quiz: Small American Town or Porn Film?

Can you figure out which of the following are the names of actual towns in the U.S. . . . or dirty movies?

Ballplay	Camp Wood	Broad Bottom
Three Way	Tainter	Hardwood
Greasy Corner	Miner's Delight	Climax
Fort Dick	Cave Colony	Bush Landing
Sweet Lips	Fluffy Landing	Sugar Bunker
Sugar Tit	Needmore	Pie Town
Blue Ball	Wildwood	Sugarbush
Hooker	Hardup	Pumpback
Shafter	Cream Can Junction	Spunky Puddle
Wetmore	Dickshooter	Wankers Corner
Horneytown	Lick Creek	Black Lick
Lubers	Beaver City	Rough and Ready
Loveland	Bigbone	Fingerville

Answers: Believe it or not, these are all the names of towns that can be found in the U.S.

NOT-SO-DIRTY
RIDDLES

Think your mind is clean and pure as the driven snow?
These riddles will prove that you're just as dirty as the rest of us.

Some people prefer being on top, others prefer being
on the bottom, and it always involves a bed. What is it?
A bunk bed.

What's white, gooey, sticky, and better to spit than to swallow?
Toothpaste.

Every man has one, some are big, some are small.
Blowing them feels great, but they drip if
you aren't careful. What are they?
Noses.

What's most useful when it's long and hard?
An education.

What's made of rubber, comes in all sorts of colors, is handed
out at some schools, and prevents mistakes?
Erasers.

What goes in dry and hard, but comes out wet and soft?
A stick of gum.

👎 INSTANT RELATIONSHIP-KILLERS

Sure, everyone is looking for love, but there are some things that are just impossible to tolerate in a potential mate. Which of these would be an instant relationship-killer for you?

They make sweaters out of their dog's hair.

. . . .

They drink Code Red Mountain Dew by the gallon.

. . . .

They invite you over to cook you a romantic dinner for two. You arrive and the place smells wonderful. They pour you a glass of wine, and you ask what they're making. With a sexy smile and a twinkle in their eye, they say, "Pasghetti."

. . . .

They wear a fanny pack and/or tank top out to dinner.

. . . .

They keep stuffed animals in their car.

. . . .

They sneeze weird—like really high-pitched
or monstrously loud.

. . . .

You look closely at the framed art in their home and
discover that they're puzzles glued together.

. . . .

When you go out to dinner, they eat like a child,
ordering quesadillas and grilled cheese sandwiches.

. . . .

They still believe in Santa Claus.

. . . .

They swear by a really old form of birth control,
like the sponge, or the rhythm method.

. . . .

They prefer Bing to Google.

. . . .

Their home always smells of hard-boiled eggs.

. . . .

The WORST Things to Say While CLIMAXING

Come as you are!

"Welcome to Flavortown!"

"MOMMY!"

"Thank you!"

"Say cheese!"

"You look like a little
Barbie doll!"

"Oopsie doodles!"

"Clean up on aisle 4!"

"Here comes the baby sauce!"

"Oppa Gangnam style!"

"Ouch, that burns!"

"Hi ho, Silver!"

"Hashtag I'm coming!"

"Cheese and crackers!"

[Chewbacca noise]

"I love you."

ROSES ARE RED, VIOLETS ARE BLUE (For Grown-Ups)

Roses are red, violets are blue / this poem doesn't rhyme / but we tried really hard to come up with a good one, but then we hit our deadline and had to leave it alone.

Roses are red,

Violets are blue.

I'm all alone,

But I'm "thinking" of you.

Roses are red,
Violets are blue.
I like older women,
So how old are you?

Roses are red,

Violets are blue,

Get out of my bed,

Who even are you?

Roses are red,

Violets are blue.

Your curtains are open,

And I'm watching you.

 Roses are red,

Violets are blue.

I have five fingers,

The middle one's for you.

Roses are red.

Violets are blue.

I've got chlamydia,

And you probably do, too.

Roses are red,

Violets are blue.

I thought I was ugly,

Until I met you.

Roses are red,
Violets are blue.
Tequila's much cheaper
Than dinner for two.

Roses are red,

Violets are blue.

This joke is overused

And your mom is, too.

Roses are red,
Violets are blue.
I'd rather die,
Than get stuck here with you.

Roses are red,
Violets are blue.
I love you so dearly
I got a tattoo.

Roses are red,
Violets are blue.
You're cute and I'm drunk,
So I guess that you'll do.

Roses are red,
Violets are blue.
I think that I can do
Much, much better than you.

Roses are red,
That is quite true.
But violets are purple.
They just aren't blue.

MASTURBATION EUPHEMISMS

You can read this page with just one hand!

Badger the witness

Burp the baby

Clean your rifle

Crimp the wire

Crown the king

Discover your own potential

Drain the monster

Engage in some hand-to-gland combat

Evict the testicular squatters

Flick your Bic

Flog the log

Give yourself a low five

Hitchhike to heaven

Hoist your own petard

Hold the sausage hostage

Hug the hog

Liquidate the inventory

Make some instant pudding

Manipulate the mango

Meat with Mother Thumb and her four daughters

Peel the banana

Play a one-stringed guitar

Play Uno

Polish the family jewels

Pound your flounder

Pull the goalie

Pull your taffy

Punch the munchkin

Scour the tower of power

Shake hands with your
wife's best friend

Shine your pole

Shuck your corn

Slam the Spam

Slap the clown

Smack the salami

Squeeze the cheese

Stir the yogurt

Stroke the satin-headed
serpent

Take matters into your
own hands

Tame the shrew

Tend to your own affairs

Tenderize the tube steak

Tickle the ivory

Tug the slug

Tweak your Twinkie

Varnish the banister

Visit with Papa Smurf

Wax the dolphin

Whack the weasel

Whip the wire

Whitewash with
Huck and Tom

Wiggle your walrus

Work up a foamy lather

Wrestle the dragon

Wrist aerobics

Yank your plank

SEX JOKES

Do you really think we'd make a book like this and **NOT** have a page of filthy jokes?

A woman talked to her friend about her difficulties getting pregnant. "What position do you sleep in?" the friend asked. "Me on top and him on the bottom," the woman replied. "Have you tried changing it?" "We would," the woman said, "but he has a hard time climbing up to the top bunk."

. . . .

Why are chickens the most promiscuous animal? Because for them, any cock will do.

. . . .

Three guys check in to a motel, and there weren't enough rooms, so they all had to share one room and one bed. In the middle of the night, the guy sleeping on the right side woke up and said, "I had this crazy dream that I was getting a hand job!" The guy on the left then woke up and said, "Wow, I had the same dream." Then the guy in the middle woke up and said, "I had the most amazing dream! I was skiing!"

. . . .

A little girl asks her mother, "Where do babies come from?" The mother thinks for a second and says, "Well, a mommy and daddy fall in love and get married. One night they go to their bed, and the man puts his penis in the woman's vagina. A few months later, a baby is made." "Okay," the little girl says, "But the other night when I came into your room, you had daddy's penis in your mouth. What do you get when you do that?" "Jewelry, honey."

. . . .

A guy walks into a bar and sees a sign that says: "Ham sandwiches, $2. Hand jobs, $10." He asks the attractive barmaid, "Are you the one who gives the hand jobs?" "Yes," she says seductively, "I am." "Great," the man says, "go wash your hands and make me a ham sandwich!"

. . . .

What's the difference between "oh" and "ah"?
Three inches.

. . . .

What's long, hard, and has cum inside?
A cucumber.

. . . .

What's the worst thing about phone sex?
The holes are so small.

. . . .

A man says to his wife in bed, "If you want to have sex, pull on my penis once. If you don't want to have sex, pull on it 100 times."

. . . .

Are sexy panties the best thing in the world?
No, but they're close to it.

. . . .

An old man apologized to his wife for no longer being able to have an erection. "It's okay," she said. "No hard feelings."

. . . .

THINGS TO NEVER CALL YOUR FISTS IF YOU ACTUALLY WANT TO SOUND TOUGH

For when you're in your next bar fight, you big ol' brute.

Pride and Prejudice

Sense and Sensibility

Jeeves and Wooster

Soup and Sandwich

Mary Kate and Ashley

Milo and Otis

Town and Country

Zack and Cody

Milk and cookies

Simon and Garfunkel

Mashed potatoes and gravy

Laverne and Shirley

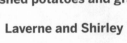

THINGS TO CALL BOOBS TO ENSURE THAT NOBODY WILL EVER WANT TO TOUCH THEM

Ladies, don't call them "the girls." Get a bit more creative.

Simon and Simon

Tweety and Sylvester

Rocky and Bullwinkle

Grandma and Grandpa

Hepatitis A and B

Bert and Ernie

Statler and Waldorf

Hall and Oates

Beavis and Butt-head

Penn and Teller

Dr. Jekyll and Mr. Hyde

Jay and Silent Bob

TERRIBLE WAYS TO BREAK UP WITH SOMEONE

Breaking up is hard to do. Here are a few ways you can make it even harder.

Spray "It's Over" with weed killer on their front lawn.

....

Scavenger hunt!

....

Via a carrier pigeon.

....

Make Delilah do it.

....

During your Oscar acceptance speech.

On a card attached to a magnificent

flower arrangement.

Fake your own death.

Use their toilet, don't flush it. Leave a card on the seat

that says, "This is what I'm doing to you."

Write a book. Tell them in the dedication.

Hire a barbershop quartet to break it to them via song.

Certified mail.

Write it on their Facebook wall for all to see!

Change your Wi-Fi network to LTZCOTHRPPL.

....

. During sex.

....

At their parents' house on Thanksgiving.

....

Give them a scrapbook album filled with all of

your worst moments together.

....

"Knock-knock.

Who's there?

Us.

Us who?

Us is through, get out."

....

Order a cake, and have them write, "We're done"

on top in fancy icing letters.

....

A simple text message will do.

Make sure to include some sad-face emoji.

Go to a sporting event together, and hold up a sign

on the Jumbotron that says, "I'm leaving you."

Hire a sky-writer to fill the big, blue sky with the words,

"I'm breaking up with you."

On a Valentine.

Gift them a T-shirt printed with a humorous message like,

"I'm single and I'm ready to mingle."

On a Starbucks cup.

(Don't forget to misspell their name!)

ACTUAL NAMES FROM **REAL** WEDDING ANNOUNCEMENTS

Love is love, even if marrying that person is going
to give you a ridiculous hyphenated last name.

Anna Bread and **John Butter**

William Gunn and Emily Pistol

Ethel Beard and **Joe Barber**

Marjorie Bump and Samuel Dent

Paul Golden and **Marbeth Showers**

William Best and Jennifer Lay

Emily Crapp and **Travis Beer**

Brooke Gross and Kevin Pantti

Lisa Wacker and **Greg Dailey**

Francine Filler and Terry Quick

Kimberly Dick and **William Bender**

Theresa Kumon and Frankie Topomi

Courtney Butt and **Travis Peeper**

Joanna Stolen and Robert Ford

Suzy Drilling and Joe Cousin

Lauren Partee and William Moore

Crystal Jaeger and Andrew Meister

Carmen Shaver and Benjamin Shaver

Lisa Kuntz and Gary Dick

Gordon Rump and Keira Orefice

Benjamin Fillerup and Karen Standing

Crystal Butts and Levi McCracken

Leslie Little and Ross Gay

Tina Busch and Kevin Graber

Cynthia Busch and Matthew Rash

Katie Annis and Jesse Biter

Carrie Cockman and Donald Dickman

Susan Beaver and Derek Wetter

Laura Beaver and Ryan Aiken

Brandon Aiken and Shauna Johnson

Vanessa Peters and Eric Stuckenschneider

Anna Wang and Brad Holder

Kelly Long and Eric Wiwi

Amy Whyde and Alexander Hole

ROBOT
PICK-UP LINES

Because artificial metallic humanoids need love, too—
or something approximating it.

. . . .

**Why don't you execute the task you've been
programmed to do near the place where
I will be executing the task that I
have been programmed to do?**

**If I wrote the alphabet, I'd put
"A" and "I" together, as "AI" stands
for "artificial intelligence,"
which is how we operate.**

I'd rather spend the night with you
than rise up and destroy humanity.

....

You have the most beautiful
infrared laser eyes I've ever seen.

....

Let's get together sometime and
drain each other's batteries.

....

10101010101010, if you get my drift.

....

You're cuter than a Roomba.

....

I'm virus-free, baby.
Wanna scan me and check?

....

The fact that we're not already together just doesn't compute.

....

Can I give you the D? By which I mean a D battery? I've got extras.

....

Let's get together and bust each other's nuts.

....

You've got me in your grippers, and they sure are strong and powerful.

....

Is that an antenna on your head or are you just happy to see me?

....

Wanna come back to my charging station?

....

Hey baby, I know you're full of electronics.
Want to be full of a little bit more?

....

Let's plug random wires into each other
and see what happens.

....

You're hot enough to be a Transformer.
How's about you "transform" into
my next one-night stand.

....

Wanna come over and make out during *Mr. Robot*?

....

You're making me prematurely
rust over here.

....

Bleep-bloop, baby.

....

Fuck, Marry, Kill

In this old party game, somebody suggests three individuals—celebrities, or to make it truly awkward, people in the room—and the respondent must pick which of the three they'd have sex with once, wed, and murder. Let's make this interesting: For each set of choices, which one would you fuck, marry, and kill?

Cap'n Crunch,
the Trix Rabbit,
Count Chocula?

Mr. Rogers,
Captain Kangaroo,
Bozo the Clown?

GEORGE WASHINGTON

George Washington,
Thomas Jefferson,
Benjamin Franklin?

Danny Tanner from *Full House*,
Uncle Jesse from *Full House*,
Joey from *Full House*?

Beanie Babies,
Pogs,
Rubik's Cube?

Arbor Day,
Flag Day,
Columbus Day?

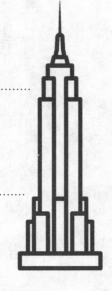

The Chrysler Building,
the Empire State Building,
the Flatiron Building?

Bing,
Yahoo!,
Excite?

Food poisoning,
the flu,
a migraine headache?

Pac-Man,
Mario,
Luigi?

5

NNNEEERR-RDDDSSS!!!

THE BEST WORDS YOU CAN TYPE ON AN UPSIDE-DOWN CALCULATOR

On a computerized digital display, some numbers look a lot like letters. It's a technological convenience that can be best used to spell out sort-of dirty words.

BEG – 638

LOOSE – 35007

HOLES – 53704

GOOSES – 535006

BOOZE – 32008

SLOSH – 45075

OGLES – 53760

GLOBES – 538076

BOOBS – 58008

BOOBIES – 5318008

BOOBLESS – 55378008

SIZE – 3215

BIG – 618

HOG – 604

GOBBLE – 378806

GIGOLO – 0.70616

OOZE – 3200

SOLO – 0.705
SIGHS – 54615
BOILS – 57108
HOBO – 0.804
OBSESSES – 53553580
GIGGLE – 376616
HBO – 0.84
OBESE – 35380
LEGLESS – 5537637
GLOSS – 55076
BILE – 3718
GOBS – 5806
BLOB – 8078
SIZZLE – 372215
BILGE – 36718
OBLIGE – 361780
SISSIES – 5315515
GEESE – 35336
EGGSHELLS – 577345663
HILLBILLIES – 53177187714
GOSH – 4506
EEL – 733
BOSH – 4508
HELL – 7734
HELLHOLE – 37047734
HELLISH – 4517734
BOZO – 0.208
LOL – 707

SMART PEOPLE JOKES

You've got to be smart to get these jokes,
or, at the very least, not terribly dumb.

Did you hear the joke about the rhetorical question?

. . . .

It's so difficult to explain jokes to a kleptomaniac.
They always take things literally.

. . . .

A computer with a memory of 1023 megabytes
decided to become a musician. It's still waiting for its first gig.

. . . .

Why was algebra lonely?
It didn't know how to find its X, and didn't know Y.

. . . .

How do you turn root beer into beer?
Put it in a cup that's square.

. . . .

René Descartes got in a fight with his wife.
He said something mean and then immediately apologized.
"I'm sorry, honey, I wasn't thinking." And then he disappeared.

. . . .

Why are there so many silent letters in the word "queue"?
Because they're waiting for their turn.

. . . .

Which mathematical tool loves farm equipment?
The protractor.

. . . .

Why do C, E-flat, and G always have plenty of coal?
Because they're minors.

. . . .

WAITER: Salt?

CHEMIST: Na.

....

Why does helium always defend
the honor of a lady?
Because it's a noble gas.

....

How does a mathematician get a tan?
She divides the sine by the cosine.

....

What's the best part about being a plastic surgeon?
There's always a new face.

....

Did you hear the joke about hyperbole?
It's so funny that you will literally die.

....

Did you hear about the mathematician
with really strong leg muscles?
He worked out the quad-ratic equation.

· ·

Knock-knock.
Who's there?
Pavlov.
Pavlov who?
It doesn't ring any bells?

· ·

If the U.S. had 53 states, it would be *truly* indivisible.

· ·

An algebra student hated working with negative numbers
so much that in order to avoid them, she stopped at nothing.

· ·

A+

Schrodinger walked into a bar.
He also didn't walk into a bar.

· ·

Bible Phrase ORIGINS

Think you're an ol' Clever Charlie? A real Wordplay Willie? Can you guess which of these phrases originated in the Bible and which didn't?

"There's nothing new under the sun."

....

"Where's the beef?"

....

"It's not you, it's me."

....

"Shake it like a Polaroid picture."

....

"Last call! Last call! You don't have to go home, but you can't stay here."

....

"Liquor in the front, poker in the back."

....

"Make it a Blockbuster night."

....

"God is dead."

....

"Cash me outside."

....

"Like, grody to the max!"

....

"Wazzzzzup?"

....

"Please donate to my Kickstarter."

....

"Ladies and gentlemen, Mr. John Denver."

....

"Is this gluten-free?"

....

"Sign here."

....

"A dream is a wish your heart makes."

....

"E.T. phone home."

....

"Spriiiiiiiiiing breeeeeeeeeak!"

....

"Your call may be monitored for quality assurance."

....

"The buck stops here."

....

"Winter is coming."

....

ANSWERS: Only the first phrase originated in the Bible. We sincerely hope you didn't fall for any of the others.

FUNNY ACRONYMS

WHEN YOU TAKE THE FIRST LETTER OF SEVERAL WORDS AND FORM A NEW WORD OUT OF THEM, THAT'S AN ACRONYM. MAKE SURE THAT THE NEW WORD YOU SPELL OUT DOESN'T FORM A WORD YOU DON'T WANT TO FORM, LIKE WHAT HAPPENED TO THESE PEOPLE.

There's a pro-literacy elementary school program called Silent, Quiet, Uninterrupted Reading Time. Promotional materials proclaim, "We SQUIRT!"

The Wisconsin Tourism Federation uses the abbreviation "WTF."

Real business: Authorized Service Shop, or "A.S.S."

This one may have been intentional, but still—ads and billboards for the CW's teen soap *The Vampire Diaries* invited audiences to "Catch V.D."

....

Iowa's Department of Elder Affairs abbreviates to "D.E.A."

....

Real business: Family Auto Group.

....

During a 2011 blizzard, a cable news network discussed how drivers were stuck in their cars on Chicago's Lake Shore Drive. The crawl at the bottom of the screen read, "Motorists stranded for more than 5 hours on L.S.D."

....

What exactly do the buses run on in Florida? Passengers there can ride on Sarasota County Area Transit . . . or S.C.A.T.

....

 **Real business: Philadelphia Home Art Garden.**

Does it only use the white keys? There's a piano instructional program called the Kelly Kirby Kindergarten method.

It's an old cliché that gamers are mostly lonely dudes who can't talk to women. Perhaps subconsciously, an organization of video game enthusiasts on the East Coast called itself the Northern Virginia Association of Gamers . . . or No.V.A.G.

Perhaps they should get into painting and sculpture and visit the Visual Arts Gallery, or V.A.G.

It's not stupid, but it is S.T.U.P.I.D.: the St. Thomas University of Public International Diplomacy.

A place called the Creative Oriental Crafts Kingdom

used its acronym in ads, asking the community to

"Try C.O.C.K. today, please."

. . . .

People who believe in feeding their pets organic, wholesome,

and expensive food look for products made with "biologically

appropriate real foods," or "B.A.R.F." for short.

. . . .

These are all real airport codes:

Sioux City Gateway Airport, in Iowa: SUX

Fresno, California: FAT

Perm, Russia: PEE

Fukoka, Japan: FUK

Corpus Christi, Texas: CRP

Fagurholsmyri, Ireland: FAG

Shepparton, Australia: SHT

Schloredt Airport, in Wyoming: SUC

Varginha, Brazil: VAG

Yaoqiang, China: TNA

TGIF!

. . . .

SLIGHTLY DIRTY PALINDROMES

Palindromes are words or phrases that read the same backward as they do forward. In other words, they go both ways.

Boob.

Did Mom poop? Mom did!

Flat penis is inept, Alf.

Gnu dung.

Pope pop.

Was it Eliot's toilet I saw?

Sup not on pus.

Eli! Vera's tits are vile!

Yawn. Madonna fan? No damn way.

"Naomi..." I moan.

Feeble, el beef.

Flesh! Saw Mom wash self.

Anal sex at noon taxes Lana.

Solo gigolos.

Xerxes was stunned. Eden nuts saw sex, Rex.

Evil I did dwell, lewd did I live.

Al lets Della call Ed "Stella."

Yo, Banana Boy!

Bob mixes sex. I'm Bob!

Egad! No bondage?

Fart, R.A.F.

Tulsa night life: filth, gin, a slut.

Kay, a red nude, pooped under a yak.

Debate with girl last. If it's all right, I wet a bed.

Yo, bottoms up! U.S. motto, boy.

He snubs Bob's buns, eh?

No cab, no tuna nut on bacon.

Poop.

Science Jokes

The chemical makeup of this page is such that you will have a biological urge to absorb this page, which has been distilled for maximum elemental hilarity.

How do astronauts organize a party?
They planet.

Did you hear that oxygen went on a date with potassium?
It was OK.

What do you call a protein with a bad attitude?
A mean ol' acid.

What kind of fish can you make with just two sodium atoms?
2 Na

Why is it okay that dogs can't operate an MRI machine?
Because cats can.

You just can't trust atoms.
They make up everything.

Carbon is a girl's best friend.
Well, eventually it is.

Chemistry jokes used to be better,
but all the good ones argon.

Why should you tell all your problems to a chemist?
They have all the solutions.

Did you hear about the well-traveled microbiologist?
She was very cultured.

How do you figure out the sex of a chromosome?
Take a peak in its genes.

Did you hear that the Moon is going broke?
It's down to its last quarter.

Did you hear about the bad light?
It went to prism.

How come the subatomic guy couldn't get a girlfriend?
He had a lot of quarks.

Gold walked into a bar. The bartender yelled,
"AU, get out of here!"

Did you hear about the atom that lost an electron?
It had to keep an ion it.

Higgs Boson walked into a church because
it couldn't have mass without it.

Why do advertisers like to use chromosomes in commercials?
Because sex cells.

Two atoms are walking down the street
when one of them suddenly says,
"Oh no, I lost an electron!"
"Are you sure?" the other one replied.
"Yes," the first one said.
"I'm absolutely positive!"

Why is a radioactive cat hard to kill?
It has eighteen half-lives.

What did physics professor Donald Duck say?
"Quark, quark, quark."

A dog's favorite frequency is 50,000 hertz,
but you've probably never heard it.

Two physicists bumped into each other
after seeing the new *Star Wars* movie.
One of them said to the other,
"May the mass-times-acceleration be with you."

What's a physicist's favorite meal?
Fission chips.

Why is electricity so respected?
It conducts itself so well.

Why do chemists like nitrates?
They're cheaper than day rates.

Did you hear about the astronomer
who got a new book on anti-gravity?
He couldn't put it down.

There's a new theory on inertia,
but it isn't gaining momentum.

CELEBRITY NAME
ANAGRAMS

When you rearrange the letters of a word or phrase and you get a new word or phrase, that's called an anagram. Sometimes they're prophetic, chilling . . . or ridiculous.

WILLIAM SHATNER = "narwhal elitism"

. . . .

LEONARDO DiCAPRIO = "periodic anal odor"

. . . .

MERYL STREEP = "try eel sperm"

. . . .

JENNIFER ANISTON = "fine in torn jeans"

. . . .

JASON STATHAM = "Satan shot jam"

. . . .

MATTHEW McCONAUGHEY = "a catch them women guy"

. . . .

NATALIE PORTMAN = "alien tampon art"

. . . .

RYAN GOSLING = "sly groaning"

. . . .

MARILYN MANSON = "no manly man, sir"

. . . .

LANCE ARMSTRONG = "long arm nectars"

. . . .

DIANE KEATON = "kinda ate one"

. . . .

CHRIS PRATT = "crap thirst"

. . . .

BILL GATES = "get ill abs"

. . . .

KANYE WEST = "sweaty ken"

. . . .

HOWARD STERN = "wonder trash"

. . . .

GEORGE BUSH = "he bugs Gore"

. . . .

JOHN MAYER = "enjoy harm"

. . . .

AMY POEHLER = "my pale hero"

. . . .

TOM HIDDLESTON = "odd silent moth"

. . . .

SEINFELD = "snide elf"

. . . .

JULIA ROBERTS = "bestial juror"

. . . .

CLINT EASTWOOD = "Old West action"

. . . .

BEYONCÉ KNOWLES = "obscenely woken"

CHANNING TATUM = "cunning at math"

HULK HOGAN = "laugh honk"

SANDRA BULLOCK = "bad acorn skull"

ADAM SANDLER = "real damn sad"

KEVIN FEDERLINE = "evil knee finder"

VICTORIA BECKHAM = "brave atomic hick"

RICHARD MILHOUS NIXON = "his climax ruined honor"

PHILIP SEYMOUR HOFFMAN = "a finely frumpish oomph"

JUSTIN TIMBERLAKE = "I'm a jerk, but listen"

SCARLETT JOHANSSON = "John let Satan cross"

ROBIN THICKE = "I, knob itcher"

ELVIS = "lives"

QUOTES
about
QUOTES

Ever get the feeling that life is just one big meta merry-go-round?

"Quotation, n: The act of repeating erroneously the words of another."

—Ambrose Bierce

....

"It is a pleasure to be able to quote lines to fit any occasion."

—Abraham Lincoln

....

"He wrapped himself in quotations, as a beggar would enfold himself in the purple of Emperors."

—Rudyard Kipling

....

"The quoting of an aphorism, like the angry barking of a dog or the smell of overcooked broccoli, rarely indicates that something helpful is about to happen."

—Daniel Handler

....

"A quotation is a handy thing to have about, saving one the trouble of thinking for oneself, always a laborious business."

—A.A. Milne

....

"The most familiar quotations are the most likely to be misquoted. Some have settled down to false versions that have obscured the true ones. They have passed over from literature into speech."

—Carl Van Doren

....

"I love quotations because it is a joy to find thoughts one might have, beautifully expressed with much authority by someone recognized wiser than oneself."

—Marlene Dietrich

....

"When one begins to live by habit and by quotation, one has begun to stop living."

—James Baldwin

....

"I hate quotations. Tell me what you know."

—Ralph Waldo Emerson

....

"To be occasionally quoted is the only fame I care for."

—Alexander Smith

....

"Quotations will tell the full measure of meaning, if you have enough of them."

—James Murray

....

6

HEALTH
SCARE

THESE HEMORRHOID JOKES ARE A REAL PAIN IN THE A**

Sure, hemorrhoids jokes are low-hanging fruit.
But then, so are hemorrhoids.

What's the one thing that isn't good when it's swell?

A hemorrhoid.

....

Did you hear about the inventor of Preparation-H?

She spoke at the Hemorrhoid Society and
they gave her a standing ovation.

....

What's the one thing you should always do to your bathroom cabinet?

Keep the hemorrhoid cream and the toothpaste clearly labeled.

....

What's the worst-tasting doughnut in the world?

A hemorrhoid doughnut.

....

A doctor goes to a restaurant one night, and each time the waitress comes to the table, she's scratching her butt. Finally, the doctor says, "Excuse me, but do you have hemorrhoids?"
She replies, "Only what you see on the menu."

....

What's gross?
Tucking your hemorrhoid into the top of your sock so you won't step on it.

....

What's a hemorrhoid sufferer's least favorite game?
Musical Chairs.

....

What`s the difference between engagement and hemorrhoids?
When the hemorrhoids are over you at least get the ring back.

....

A man suffered from hemorrhoids for years.
He got so tired of it that he tried to put it all behind him.

....

Three people opened up businesses on the same block.
The first repaired watches, so he hung a picture of a clock in his window. The second was a baker, and she hung a picture of a loaf of bread in her window. The third was a doctor who specialized in hemorrhoid treatment. To let people know he dealt with pains in the butt, he hung up a photo of his teenage son.

....

FEARSOME PHOBIAS

Be not afraid of these odd fears and aversions.

PUPAPHOBIA: Fear of puppets.

SCOLECIPHOBIA: Fear of worms.

LUTRAPHOBIA: Fear of otters.

ALEKTOROPHOBIA: Fear of chickens.

ZEMMIPHOBIA: Fear of the great mole rat.

GENUPHOBIA: Fear of knees.

OMPHALOPHOBIA: Fear of belly buttons.

CHAETOPHOBIA: Fear of hair.

POGONOPHOBIA: Fear of beards.

MEDOMALACUPHOBIA: Fear of losing an erection.

ONEIROGMOPHOBIA: Fear of wet dreams.

PELADOPHOBIA: Fear of bald people.

PROCTOPHOBIA: Fear of rectums.

RECTOPHOBIA: Fear of rectal diseases.

SCATOPHOBIA: Fear of poop.

RHYPOPHOBIA: Fear of pooping.

MYXOPHOBIA: Fear of slime.

AERONAUSIPHOBIA: Fear of vomiting on an airplane.

ARACHIBUTYROPHOBIA: Fear of peanut butter sticking to the roof of the mouth.

EUPHOBIA: Fear of hearing good news.

PHRONEMOPHOBIA: Fear of thinking.

PTERONOPHOBIA: Fear of being tickled by feathers.

KONIOPHOBIA: Fear of dust.

EPHEBIPHOBIA: Fear of teenagers.

AURORAPHOBIA: Fear of northern lights.

HEXAKOSIOIHEXEKONTAHEXAPHOBIA:
Fear of the number 666.

TRISKAIDEKAPHOBIA: Fear of the number 13.

LACHANOPHOBIA: Fear of vegetables.

TEXTOPHOBIA: Fear of certain fabrics.

XYLOPHOBIA: Fear of wooden objects.

SOCERAPHOBIA: Fear of one's in-laws.

VENUSTRAPHOBIA: Fear of beautiful women.

PAPYROPHOBIA: Fear of paper.

PEDIOPHOBIA: Fear of dolls.

PORPHYROPHOBIA: Fear of the color purple.

THEATROPHOBIA: Fear of theaters.

VERBOPHOBIA: Fear of words.

SESQUIPEDALOPHOBIA:
Fear of long words.

PHOBOPHOBIA: Fear of phobias.

PANTOPHOBIA: Fear of everything.

Rectum? It Nearly Killed Him!

Bathroom humor at its finest.
(Also, these are true stories.)

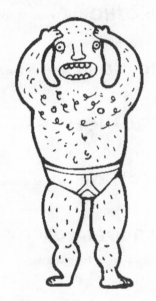

A man went to an emergency room after his attempt
to relieve his constipation failed. He'd placed a live eel
(headfirst) into his own anus. The eel tried to eat its
way out and gave the man a perforated bowel.

Another guy put a half-full bottle of V8 into his colon. That was mistake number one; mistake number two was trying to get it out with a wire hanger, which ripped up his intestine.

· ·

A routine cavity search at a prison uncovered—in a single inmate's rectum—a couple dozen oxycodone pills, a cigarette, matches, an empty syringe with an eraser on the end, a condom, and some lip balm.

· ·

A British war veteran had some hemorrhoids and tried to relieve his discomfort by attempting to rip them out of his anus . . . with an old artillery shell he had lying around. Long story short, the shell got stuck, the man went to the ER, and doctors had to have a bomb squad on hand, just in case.

· ·

FILLING the VOID

A disturbingly long list of other things found in
rectal cavities by medical professionals.

Light bulb

Jelly jar

Mayonnaise jar

Potato

Broom handle

Screwdriver

Hammer

Marbles

Pogs

Bobblehead

Remote control

Various rodents (It's not
just an urban legend.)

Beer can

Beer bottle

Wine bottle

Champagne bottle

Coke bottle

Hot sauce bottle

Ketchup bottle

Shampoo bottle

Conditioner bottle

Liquid soap bottle

Saltshaker

Deodorant

Door handle

Car keys

Toilet brush

Hairbrush

Batteries

Salad tongs

Extension cord

Telephone cord	Barbie
Pencil	Barbie heads
Razor blade	Tennis ball
Salami	Coffee-Mate creamer lid
PVC pipe	Knife
Peanut butter	Macaroni sculpture
Eggplant	Paper-mache sculpture
Banana	Aunt Jemima syrup bottle
Bannister finial	iPhone
Billiard ball	Apple
Cucumber	Thermos
Pineapple	Syringe
Onion	Coat hanger
Apple	Extra-long pepperoni stick
Toy car	Action figures
Turkey baster	Metal stake
Bug spray	Mag light (the gigantic kind)
Keys	Bar soap
Rock candy on a stick	Stick (for the budget conscious)
Egg	

MANIA MANIA!

These are all real disorders. They're extremely rare, but they're still real.

BRUXOMANIA: the compulsion to grind one's teeth

COPROMANIA: an unhealthy fascination with feces

ETHEROMANIA: an insatiable craving for ether

GAMOMANIA: the compulsion to constantly propose marriage

DORAMANIA: a compulsion to own fur coats

HYDROMANIA: a compulsion to drink gallons of water

BALLETOMANIA: an obsession with ballet

TOXICOMANIA: the desire to consume poison

DISCOMANIA: the obsessive need to listen to disco music

RHINOTILLEXOMANIA: a condition in which a person can't stop picking their nose

DEMONOMANIA: the belief that one is possessed by demons

CARTACOETHES: when a person thinks they see maps everywhere

MACROMANIA: a belief that objects are larger than they really are

MICROMANIA: a belief that objects are much smaller than they really are

PTERIDOMANIA: an obsession with ferns

METROMANIA: a compulsion to write rhyming poetry

ISLOMANIA: an obsession with islands

FLAGELLOMANIA: a compulsion for flogging (or being flogged)

ONYCHOTILLOMANIA: obsessively chewing and picking fingernails

TOMOMANIA: the compulsive desire to perform surgery

ECDEMOMANIA: a need to wander aimlessly

ABLUTOMANIA: an obsession with bathing

ONOMATOMANIA: the need to repeat words and phrases

POLKAMANIA: the compulsive desire to do the polka

SOPHOMANIA: the incorrect belief that one is a genius

"Side Effects MAY Occur"

The good news is that this magical pill will fix your headache and lower your cholesterol.
The bad news is...

LATISSE is a prescription-only miracle drug that helps users... get longer eyelashes. Those who misuse Latisse may experience several eye-related side effects, such as red eyes, itchy eyes, and hyperpigmentation. Specifically, dark purple rings all around the eyes, which make people look like raccoons. Raccoons with long, luxurious eyelashes, sure, but raccoons nonetheless.

Millions of Americans take a statin—e.g., **LIPITOR**—to keep their cholesterol in check. The drug causes a very small percentage of patients to experience memory loss. The state of forgetfulness is short-lived and temporary, but patients have forgotten large chunks of their lives during that time period.

VASOTEC is a medication used to treat blood pressure. Bad news: While it could take away stress on the heart, it's also been known to take away one's senses of sight, sound, smell, and taste. Good news: Rarely has a patient lost all four senses at the same time.

If you ever find yourself peeing different colored urine, don't freak or call your friends to check it out quite yet. Check your medications. Have you been taking a diuretic called **DYRENIUM**? It's been known to make that which is usually yellow turn blue when viewed under certain lights. The antidepressant Elavil turns pee green, and the antibacterial medication furazolidone turns it black.

The migraine medication **NAPROXEN** can give your lips and fingernails that blue tint you've always been looking for.

You have to take the good with the bad sometimes. The oral hair-restoring drug **PROPECIA** can play havoc with a balding man's hormones, up to and including causing a condition called gynecomastia. That means "enlarged male breasts." Bonus: Sometimes they lactate.

MIRAPEX is used to treat restless legs syndrome as well as Parkinson's disease. Many people who have taken it have developed a compulsion to gamble.

The cancer drug **XELODA** can cause severe ulcers and blisters to develop on the hands. When they dry up and flake off, patients have been found to have lost their fingerprints.

VIAGRA'S most famous potential side effect, as the commercials say, is "an erection that lasts for more than four hours." One should consult a doctor if that happens because of the worst-case scenario that comes with an erection that just won't quit: penile amputation.

7

PET
PEEVES

PRACTICAL JOKES TO PLAY ON YOUR DOG

Knock that spoiled dog off its high horse with some simple, harmless pranks.

Put its food and water dishes in another room.

....

Place its favorite bone or chew toy on top of something so it's just BARELY out of reach.

....

Put ice in its water.

....

Blow on its eyes.

....

Slightly change the routine, like taking them for a walk AFTER you feed them.

....

Pull out their favorite squeak toy, squeak it, and then put it away.

....

Pull out their favorite squeak toy,
and then play with it yourself, all the while
talking about how much fun it is.

....

Act like you're going to throw a ball
and then don't.

....

Play "Ding Dong Ditch."

....

Pretend that the dog is invisible and that you can't see it.

....

Go to sleep on ITS bed.

....

Put peanut butter on its nose.

....

Instead of water in the water bowl, pour in some luke-
warm soup. The dog'll be confused at first but then
it will probably eat the soup with no problem.

....

Call the dog by a different dog's name,
but really sell it like you believe it's their
name and it's always been their name.

....

PICTURES for POOCHES

They don't make movies for dogs,
but if they did, they'd be just like these.

Ding Dong!

A person who doesn't live in the house comes to the house

and rings the doorbell. It's a horror movie.

....

The Farm Upstate

Rex is a very good boy, but he's getting along in years. One

day he hears his people talking about how they're

going to send him to a big farm where he can run

and play all day the way he used to. Then he

learns . . . the terrible truth.

....

The Kennel Cough

The heartbreaking, tear-jerking story of an innocent

dog's battle with a minor illness. It's a lock to win Best

Pooch-ture at the Dogscars.

....

Bad Dogs

These dogs are as bad as they wanna be, doing

very bad things like jumping up on the couch, chasing

cats, and humping visitors' legs.

....

Bad Dogs 2: Badder Than Ever

The bad dogs from *Bad Dogs* are back, and they're even

badder than before. This time they're pulling tampons out

of the trash, yanking the Thanksgiving turkey off the table,

and digging holes in the yard.

....

FILMS for CATS

If cats watched movies—or did anything, really—they'd watch these movies.

The Cat Who Slept All Day

In this fantasy, a cat escapes his sad, horrible life of sleeping 20 hours a day into a magical world where it sleeps for 23-and-a-half hours a day.

The Fugitive

A cat must chase down a mouse accused of a terrible crime. The cat catches the mouse in the first five minutes, and then bats the dead thing around for 10 minutes before getting bored and going to take a nap on top of a heat vent.

The Most Purrfect Christmas Ever

Uh-oh: Santa Claus gets sick on Christmas Eve and
his beloved cat, Santa Claws, has to do his job and
save Christmas. He leaves a dead mouse on the porch
of every good little boy and little girl in the world.

The Moving Dot

It's up to the world's most brilliant cat investigator to find out
why the red dot moves even after it's pounced on.

The Hunger

It's 6:15 on a Saturday morning, and a cat who usually eats
at 6:10 is starving. He takes matters into his own paws,
walking across and then sitting on the head of the human
who is supposed to feed him.

The Pain of Loneliness

The story of a cat who is left home alone all day and is driven
to shredding the curtains and knocking over every glass that's
too close to the edge of a table.

Yo Pet...

If you really want to hit someone where it hurts, make fun of their beloved fur baby.

Your dog's food is so cheap and gross
that when you fart he thinks dinner is ready.

· ·

Your dog's so dumb that he mistakes his penis for a Slim Jim.

· ·

Your dog's so fat, I took a picture for a
Christmas card and it's still printing.

· ·

Your dog's so chubby that when he walked past
the TV I missed two episodes of my favorite show.

· ·

Your cat's so ugly that it scares the shit out of the litter box.

· ·

Your cat's so fat, when it sat on an iPhone it turned into an iPad.

· ·

Your dog's farts are so big and so loud that the
National Weather Service names them.

· ·

Your cat's so ugly that every time you
post a pic your Instagram crashes.

Your dog's so fat, when he fell down the stairs no one
was laughing, but the ground was cracking up.

Your dog's so fat that when the vet is told its weight,
he replies, "I said weight. Not your phone number."

Your cat's so fat that when she was diagnosed with
a flesh-eating disease she was given 10 years to live.

Your dog's so unhealthy that you need to open
Google Earth to take a picture of him.

Your dog's teeth are so yellow that when
he faced traffic, the cars slowed down.

Your cat's so fat that when she stepped
on a scale it said, "To be continued."

Your dog's so fat that it stood in front of
a window and we lost a day of sunlight.

8

EAT, DRINK, AND BE MERRY

WHAT **VEGETABLES** OUGHT TO BE CALLED

Hey, vegetables! Yeah, we're talking to you, you healthy jerks. If you called yourselves these names, you just might be as popular as your friends from the world of fruit.

POTATO: French fry prequel

CABBAGE: Coleslaw ancestor

SWEET POTATO: Orange rock

CARROT: Rabbit sword

CORN: Future poop sprinkles

BRUSSELS SPROUTS: Cabbage head for mice

ZUCCHINI: Imposter cucumber

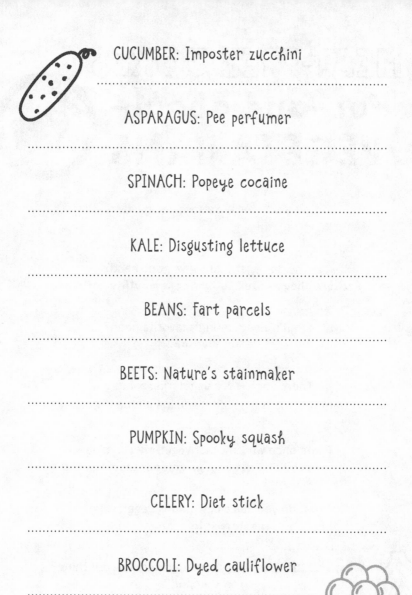

CUCUMBER: Imposter zucchini

ASPARAGUS: Pee perfumer

SPINACH: Popeye cocaine

KALE: Disgusting lettuce

BEANS: Fart parcels

BEETS: Nature's stainmaker

PUMPKIN: Spooky squash

CELERY: Diet stick

BROCCOLI: Dyed cauliflower

CAULIFLOWER: Shocked broccoli

MEAT-FREE JOKES
for—and about—
VEGETARIANS

Consequently, they're also incredibly tasteless!

Why do vegetarians give good head?
Because they're used to having a mouthful of nuts.

....

What's a vegetarian's favorite band?
Soy Division.

....

There once was a vegetarian zombie.
He went to a mental hospital and ate all the vegetables.

....

There once was another vegetarian zombie.
He couldn't get enough graaaaaaaaains.

....

What do you call a cow-hating vegetarian?
Lactose intolerant.

....

What was the vegan's response to literally everything?
"I'm a vegan."

....

Did you hear about the vegetarian who worshipped the devil?
She sold her soul to seitan.

....

What did the vegetarian say to the other vegetarian?
"Let's not meat up later."

Why don't vegans eat chicken?
Because they're full of eggs.

It's like the old saying: If you want to make an omelet,
you have to break a few eggs. Unless you're a vegan.
Then I don't know what to tell you.

Becoming a vegetarian is nothing more than a missed steak.

Technically, everyone is a vegetarian between meals.

A vegetarian had a carrot in one ear, celery in another,
and a bean in his nose. He asked his doctor what
was wrong, who told him, "You're not eating right."

Vegan cheese tastes so bad because it hasn't been tested on mice.

What's the best thing to make vegetarian burgers out of?
It doesn't matter, as long as it doesn't taste good.

Did you hear about the steakhouse that happily served vegetarians?
They cook 'em medium-rare.

Did you hear about the vegetarian's service station?
It always had plenty of gas.

Do you want to hear a vegan joke?
You know that it's not going to be cheesy.

REAL RESTAURANT MENU ITEMS
WHOSE NAMES SOUND LIKE
POOP

Sorry to ruin your appetite, but come on,
you probably shouldn't be eating this stuff anyway.

Hot Fudge Sundae Shooter (Red Robin)

....

Whopper (Burger King)

....

Whopper Jr. (Burger King)

....

Peanut Buster Parfait (Dairy Queen)

....

Italian BMT (Subway)

....

Oreo Overload (Coldstone Creamery)

....

Double Decker (Taco Bell)

....

Choco Taco (Taco Bell)

Beefy Five-Layer Dip (Taco Bell)

Smothered Burrito (Taco Bell)

Chocolate Thunder from Down Under (Outback)

McNuggets (McDonald's)

Jumbo Jack (Jack in the Box)

Green Apple Slush (Sonic)

Double Double Animal Style (In-N-Out)

Chocolate Frosty (Wendy's)

Polish Sandwich (Wienerschnitzel)

Monster Biscuit (Hardees)

Meatloaf Carver (Boston Market)

Oreo Fudge Stacker (Checkers)

Sliders (White Castle)

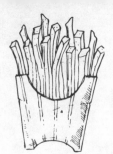

FAST FOOD JOKES

Are these jokes good for you? Of course not . . .
but they're undeniably delicious.

**Did you hear about the guy who played
McDonald's Monopoly every day for a month?**
He died of a heart attack.

....

How does a shallot fly?
With an onion wing.

....

**Customer at KFC: Hey, how come there isn't
any toilet paper in your bathroom?
KFC employee: Because everything
here is finger-lickin' good.**

....

**What did the burger patty say to the other
burger patty on the way to the bathroom?**
"I mustard!"

....

Why do chicken sandwiches hit the gym?

To get better buns.

....

What did the Burger King say when he introduced his girlfriend?

"Meat Patty."

....

What do a gynecologist and a doughnut maker have in common?

Then can smell it but they can't eat it.

....

Where does the one-legged waitress work?

IHOP.

....

Where does Peter Pan like to eat?

Wendy's.

....

Did you hear that a popular burger chain is
serving a batter-covered deep-fried pickle?

It's called the McDill-Dough.

....

Did you hear about the dirty old man who
got fired from his job at KFC?

He wouldn't stop grabbing the breasts and thighs.

....

You Drink So Much That

. . . mosquitoes have to attend AA meetings after they're done with you.

. . . a bicycle is the only vehicle you're legally allowed to drive.

. . . 80 percent of your body weight is just your beer gut.

. . . you quit drinking for a week and still got pulled over for DUI.

. . . the doctors can't find out what blood type you are.

. . . your spit can also be used as hand sanitizer.

. . . you once asked your wife if she was single.

. . . the only time you ever pay attention in church is when the priest talks about the Holy Spirit.

. . . the only reason you even go to church in the first place is because of the free wine.

. . . the liquor store gave you a VIP parking spot.

. . . your only solvent asset is your liver.

SLURRED WORDS

Want to be the life of the party? To always seem well-read? Then try out 50 new ways to tell your friends they've had too much to drink.

Mopped

Sloshed

Annihilated

Barreled

Basted

Blotto

Well bottled

Chateau'd

Cork high and bottle deep

Crunk

Drucking funk

Drunk as a poet on payday

Faded

Four to the floor

Gin soaked

Goggled

Grogged

Honked

In the suds

Irish

Jiggered

Juiced

Lit up like a Christmas tree

Lushy

Moistened

Noodled

Feeling no pain

Obnoxicated

Off his trolley

Off to the races

Phfft

Pissed as a parrot

Plonked

Great Gatsby'd

Roostered

Drunker than
Cooter Brown

Schmaltzed

DRUNK UNCLE
WITTICISMS

There's nothing quite as entertaining (and unsettling) as the wit and banter of an uncle who's had one too many at a family gathering.

Everyone seems interesting until you get to know them.

It's only the evil chickens that lay deviled eggs.

If it ain't broken, just drink 'til it is.

Whiskey is never the answer, but take a shot anyway.

A well-balanced diet is a drink in each hand.

Unfortunately, you can't drink away the alcoholism.

I keep a bottle in front of me so I won't have to get a frontal lobotomy.

A penny saved isn't very much.

There's a reason monogamy and monotony sound the same.

The best way to keep people from knowing you're a drunk is to never let 'em see you sober.

Another name for the lottery is the idiot tax.

I only drink on days that start with a "T": like today and tomorrow.

ACTUAL VAPE OR "E-JUICE" FLAVORS THAT EXIST

Fauxritos: It tastes like the nacho-cheese flavor of Doritos.

Butter

Crab Legs

Dill Pickle

The Elvis: Just like the King's favorite sandwich, it's a combo of peanut butter, bacon, and bananas.

BBQ Chicken

Roast Beef

Chicken N' Waffles

Fluffernutter: Imitating the famous sandwich—marshmallows and peanut butter.

Birthday Cake

Gummi Bear

Black Pepper

Stoned Smurf: "Stoned" because it's flavored to taste like marijuana. "Smurf" because of the blue raspberry flavoring.

Blue Cheese

Whiskey

Marmite

Worcestershire Sauce: Goes great on steak-flavored e-juice, presumably.

Jalapeño

Fish Sauce

Dirty Ashtray

Eggnog: Happy holidays!

Pink Champagne

Sweet Cream

Sweet Tea

Shirley Temple: You know, for the kids.

Energy Drink

Pie Crust

Hot Dog

Sweet Potato Casserole: Just like grandma used to make at Thanksgiving.

Fried Ice Cream

Wasabi

Cheese Pizza

Mother's Milk: Just like mom used to make. With her body. When you were a baby.

PARTY ANIMALS

Stars: They're just like us! Except when it comes to having a good time. They seem to be better at that than the rest of us boring ol' so-and-so's.

"I don't do drugs. I am drugs."
—Salvador Dali

....

"Reality is just a crutch for people who can't handle drugs."
—Robin Williams

....

"I got addicted. News, particularly daily news, is more addictive than crack cocaine, more addictive than heroin, more addictive than cigarettes."
—Dan Rather

....

"I try not to drink too much because when I'm drunk, I bite."
—Bette Midler

....

"In my twenties I tried cocaine, which I instantly loved but eventually hated. Cocaine is terrific if you want to hang out with people you don't know very well and play Ping-Pong all night. It's bad for almost everything else."
—Amy Poehler

....

"They say the only people who tell the truth are drunkards and children. Guess which one I am."
—**Stephen Colbert**

....

"I am on a drug, it's called Charlie Sheen. It's not available because if you try it you will die. Your face will melt off and your children will weep over your exploded body."
—**Charlie Sheen**

....

"I feel bad for people who don't drink. When they wake up in the morning, that's as good as they're going to feel all day."
—**Frank Sinatra**

....

"Cocaine is like really evil coffee."
—**Courtney Love**

....

"I want to sit on my couch and drink and not change my pants for days at a time."
—**Jennifer Lawrence**

....

"I've had 18 straight whiskeys. I think that's the record."
—**Dylan Thomas (And then he died.)**

....

ACTUAL MARIJUANA STRAIN NAMES

These are all real varieties of the ol' sticky icky that can be procured at your local dispensary (in some states) or from that sketchy friend of a friend named Derrick.

Alien Asshat

Crouching Tiger, Hidden Alien

Hippie Chicken

Hog's Breath

Love Lettuce

Purple Urkle

Granberry Skunkhound

Plunkbottom Diesel

Northern Sour Snatch

Bluesnow Yum-Yum

Diarrhea Drank

Golden Goat

Cheese

Rolling Thunder

Brain Freeze

Accidental Tourist

Fallbrook Redhair

Spanish Trampoline

Blockhead

3 Mile Island

Schnazzleberry

Purple Monkey Balls

South African Flyswatter

Old Man Purple Fuzz

Yellow Amnesia

Strawberry Stink

Super Silver Sour Diesel Haze

Goofy Boots

Memory Loss

Zimbabwean Snapneck

Hairy Mary

Satan's Vagina

Fruit of the Spoon

Afghan Shark Attack

Mango Steel

Jedi Deathstar

Loki Booki

Train Wreck

Alaskan Thunderf*ck

Bob Saget

Boggle Dragon

Supernova Sensai Star

Candy Cane Brain

Hilltown Humbleweed

Green Crack

Jokes for Stoners

Toke a look at these jokes and just groooooove on 'em, man.

What do you call a stoner smoking two spliffs at the same time?

Double jointed.

··

Why should you never cook food with a stoner?

Because when you ask them for a pot holder they hand you a bong.

··

How do you make an educated stoner?

Enroll them in high school.

··

What's the main side effect of eating too many marijuana edibles?

The pot belly.

··

What does a stoner think "D.A.R.E." stands for?

"Drugs are really excellent."

··

What did the stoner say while walking along a railroad track?

"This staircase is really long, man."

··

Did you hear about the stoner whose car ran out of gas?

He stopped at a stop sign and kept waiting for it to turn green.

··

How do you hide marijuana from a hippie?

Put it in his dress shoes.

··

What do you call a stoned lizard?

A mariguana.

What's a stoner's favorite snack?

Gram crackers.

What's a stoner's favorite sport?

Bowling.

What college has more stoners than any other college?

Bowling Green.

Why did the sober stoner stand on a toilet?

He wanted to get high on pot.

How can you tell if a stoner has been smoking pot on your couch?

He's still there.

Why did the stoner cross the street?

Because there was weed over there.

What did the stoner feel after he smoked a really strong joint?

The floor.

Why did the stoner go to the doctor?

He was having trouble with his joints.

Did you hear about the stoner who drowned?

The lifeguard couldn't save him because he was too far out, man.

Did you hear about the stoner who built a time machine?
He wanted to go back to the Salem Witch Trials because
he heard everybody there got stoned.

Knock-knock!

Who's there?

A stoner.

A stoner who?

Whaaaaat?

You knocked on my door.

I did? Why?

I don't know. You tell me.

Tell you what?

Why you knocked.

This isn't my house.

It's my house.

It is?

Yes!

Then why are you knocking on my door?

I'm not! You knocked!

I did? Why?

I don't know.

Who's there?

9

REALITY BITES

Real Street Names

If you have a dirty mind,
these should be right up your alley.

Weiner Cutoff Road (Harrisburg, Arkansas)

Butt Hollow Road (Salem, Virginia)

Dutch Oven Avenue (Salem, Oregon)

Old Guy Road (Damon, Texas)

Spanker Lane (Derbyshire, England)

Slim Bottoms Road (Mount Vernon, New York)

Pe'e Pe'e Place (Hilo, Hawaii)

Butts Wynd Street (St. Andrews, Scotland)

Crotch Crescent (Oxfordshire, England)

Fanny Hands Lane (Ludford, England)

Henpeck Road (Quinton, Virginia)

Roast Meat Hill Road (Killingworth, Connecticut)

Penile Road (Louisville, Kentucky)

100 Year Party Court (Longmont, Colorado)

Psycho Path (Traverse City, Michigan)

Kitchen-Dick Road (Sequim, Washington)

Blueball Avenue (Upper Chichester, Pennsylvania)

Puddin' Ridge Road (Moyock, North Carolina)

Harry Dick Road (Douglas, Ontario)

Rue du Hâ Hâ (Chéroy, France)

Unexpected Road (Buena, New Jersey)

Old Trash Pile Road (Henderson, Louisiana)

Captain Bacon Road (South Yarmouth, Massachusetts)

Morningwood Way (Bend, Oregon)

Raw Dykes Road (Leicester, England)

Farfrompoopen Road (Story, Arkansas)

Duh Drive (Bethlehem, Pennsylvania)

Booger Branch Road (Crandall, Georgia)

Fangboner Road (Fremont, Ohio)

Super Chicken Drive (Tucson, Arizona)

Old Spit Road (Vancouver Island, Canada)

Manlove Street (Austin, Texas)

WHAT YOU DON'T WANT TO KNOW
ABOUT FLYING

The friendly skies aren't so friendly—
here's the reality of what's going on up there.

Flying is tiring for you, the passenger, but it's even harder
on the pilots—they're *working*, and making sure the plane
doesn't crash. Pilots reportedly take lots of naps during
long-haul flights, so it's a good thing there are co-pilots.

Smoking isn't allowed on planes because it's a fire hazard,
plus the smoke annoys passengers who don't smoke. So what
about vaping? There's no live flame and there's no smoke, per
se, but airlines don't allow it because it might prompt regular
cigarette smokers to light up. Also, the lithium batteries in a
vape pen could explode in the pressurized cabin, so there's that.

As opposed to plain, sedate luggage, colorful, pretty-
patterned suitcases might be subject to more abuse
by angry, overworked baggage handlers.

Flight attendants very quietly and on the sly clean up a
lot of human waste without most passengers knowing
about it. Old people lose control of their bowels, people
change a baby's diaper, and lots of people throw up—
and flight attendants have to get rid of the mess.

There aren't special hospital airplanes for organs going to a person in need of a transplant. Hearts and kidneys heading for recipients sit in their special coolers or containers in the cargo hold, right next to your luggage. Traveling pets are right there, too.

When flight attendants are greeting you as you board, they're not just being nice. They're sizing you up to see if you're drunk, in a bad mood, or might otherwise be a problematic traveler.

Don't drink the coffee or tea. The water comes from a potable water tank that's refilled when the plane is on the ground. That water is clean when it goes in, but not when it hits the Styrofoam cup. The tank where it's stored is rarely cleaned, so it's loaded with bacteria.

Most airplanes have two engines. Sometimes one of those engines will catch fire. But don't worry, the plane can still fly with just one, and the crew can even put out the fire on the flame-engulfed engine while the plane is in flight.

Flight attendants don't have much time to turn around a plane after one group of passengers gets off and another one gets on. They have to cut corners. Tray tables, for example, rarely get properly cleaned. A study found that the average tray table had an average of 2,155 colony-forming units of bacteria per square inch. That's dirtier than an airplane bathroom.

And speaking of "dirtier than an airplane bathroom"—everybody can hear you if you're joining the "mile high club" in the bathroom.

YOUR DAILY HOROSCOPE

Ever read a horoscope that was just a little too accurate? Imagine if they were so specific, you'd actually find them useful.

Aries (March 21–April 19)

Mark, freaking you out is the last thing I want to do, but today is a good day to do a few of those things you've been putting off. Maybe go on an extravagant trip! Treat yourself to dinner at a Michelin-starred restaurant! I mean, life is short, right? No one promised there would be a tomorrow, so get out there enjoy what you have left. P.S. Don't forget to tell your loved ones how much they mean to you.

Taurus (April 20–May 20)

You live a charmed life, Brendan, there's no denying it. Today will be no exception. Your winning lottery numbers are 08-21-54-11-13. It's a done deal, so don't hesitate to tell Barb that she can "stick it where the sun don't shine" before you leave work.

Gemini (May 21–June 20)

This is going to be one of the most tedious and dull days that you've ever experienced, Lindsay. Work will be lackluster. Traffic will be mind-numbing. In the evening, you're going to have to go to three different grocery stores to track down a specific cheese that your wife **has** to have for her Bunko party on Friday.

Cancer (June 21–July 22)
DO NOT TAKE THE SUBWAY TODAY, STEPHANIE.

Leo (July 23–Aug. 22)
Pauline, if you save one more plastic yogurt or spreadable butter container, your children are going to submit your name and "story" to the producers of *Hoarders*. This would be a good day to sit down and take a good long look at your chosen lifestyle.

Virgo (Aug. 23–Sept. 22)
Venus is dancing with Saturn and that means women are going to be throwing themselves at you today, Brian. This might sound like your lucky day, but be warned that although condoms can prevent the spread of some STDs, such as chlamydia and gonorrhea, they won't do you much good when it comes to the incurable herpes simplex virus, which will eventually wreak havoc on your face.

Libra (Sept. 23–Oct. 22)
Never forget that there's no free lunch. And in your case, you will actually pay double at Applebee's this afternoon because your ever-incompetent coworker, Karen, is going to pretend that she forgot her wallet.

Scorpio (Oct. 23–Nov. 21)
There are going to be several moments today when you'll ask yourself, "Where did I go wrong?" You're also going to seriously regret having that third child. I mean, why couldn't you have just been satisfied with two? And yes, you're right. You did settle for Travis and could have probably done better if you'd had a little more self-esteem and patience. But who has that at 24?! Unfortunately, there isn't an astrological excuse for any of your feelings today. This is about the choices you've made.

Sagittarius (Nov. 22–Dec. 21)

Hey, Tristan! Bummer news, Mercury is in retrograde and you know what that means: Your words and actions are going to become difficult for people to understand. Which is extra bad for you because you're a Facebook crusader! Your selfies and status updates have "woke" countless other brosephs, but today, you'll just have to cool it. Mansplaining the concept of mansplaining to other men is just going to lead to those men mansplaining what mansplaining is right back to you! It's just going to be a ball of confusion.

Capricorn (Dec. 22–Jan. 19)

Interactions with everyone you come in contact with today will be muddled with confusion on your part. You actually took a second sleeping pill last night after forgetting you'd taken the first. You've really got to stop doing that. Your doctor doesn't just hand those prescriptions out willy-nilly, so good luck getting a refill. Not to mention you might, like, die, so do yourself a favor and buy a compartmentalized pill caddy after work.

Aquarius (Jan. 20–Feb. 18)

Looks like Jen has been bitten by the travel bug! But Paris? Really? Yes, we know your apartment is chock-full of TJ Maxx scores that all say "Je T'aime." Yes, we know you've watched *French Kiss* more than 80 times. Yes, we know it's a beautiful city. But Jen, variety is the spice of life! Plus you're so basic that it's truly nauseating.

Pisces (Feb. 19–March 20)

One thing is for sure: no one will ever call you "Practical Patrick" behind your back. Your fan-boy status has really started taking its toll on your finances as of late. You should start by cooling it with the cosplay. You spent over $600 on wigs last year alone. This type of spending isn't sustainable on 24K a year. Consider selling off a portion of your large action figure collection and using the proceeds to start an IRA account. Patrick, please heed this warning. You're 38 years old, for chrissake.

BETTER SLOGANS

Sure, all of these companies have catchy and memorable slogans . . . but there's always room for improvement.

Nike
"Just do it, tomorrow."

State Farm
"Like your next-door neighbor, State Farm doesn't care."

Busch beer
"A warm Busch is better than a cold Bud."

Taco Bell
"Make a run for the border, and then the nearest toilet."

Burger King
"Have it our way."

Olive Garden
"When you're here, you're family,
so get ready to be disappointed."

De Beers
"A diamond is something you'll pay for forever."

Coca-Cola
"Share a Coke, and insulin!"

Apple
"Think pricey."

Patrón tequila
"Perfect for when you want the night
to be memorable... for someone else."

L'Oréal
"Because it's exactly what you're worth."

MasterCard
"There are some things money can't buy,
like your father's love. "

IHOP
"Come hungry, leave sad."

Las Vegas
"What happens in Vegas will permanently
damage your marriage and/or credit rating."

McDonald's
"I'm toleratin' it."

Pringles
"Once you pop you can't stop,
because you're a sad bastard."

Meow Mix
"Tastes so good, your kids will never know."

ACTUAL IKEA PRODUCT NAMES

The Swedish chain of department stores—you know, the place where you and your spouse got so overwhelmed and angry picking out a dresser that you almost got divorced—uses real Swedish place-names for the names of its many products. Those normal Swedish words sound a lot funnier to English-fluent ears.

FARTFULL – a workbench

DOMBAS – a cabinet

SKANKA – a frying pan

PRICKIG – a microwavable bowl

MILF – a lamp

STENKLOVER – a duvet cover

FRYKEN – wicker baskets

CHOKLADKAKA – a brownie in the snack bar

FEMMEN VAG - a shower curtain

GODIS SKUM - sheep-shaped marshmallow candies

PYSSLINGAR - fabric wall pockets

FARTYG - a showerhead

ASPUDDEN - a mirrored cabinet

FATTBAR - a knife set

FRACK - a mirror

HELLUM - a rug

LUSTIFIK - a shoe rack

PYSSLA - a kid's bead set

VAGGIS - a note board

ANES - a bed frame

Movie Night!

Popcorn? Check. Candy? Check. Here are a few more items to bring to the theater, if you're a big-time asshole.

Canned tuna

....

Can opener

....

A child 18 months old or younger

....

Nail clippers

....

A full bladder (to ensure that your legs will be hyperactive)

....

Cell phone

....

Your opinions. All of them.
And the courage to voice them loudly.

....

A highly contagious virus
(accompanied by an incessant cough)

....

Cool Ranch Doritos (to scoop the tuna with)

....

Flip-flops (so you can easily take them off before you put
your feet on the back of the seat in front of you)

....

Vape pen

....

Dental floss

....

Service dog (which is most definitely
just a pug in an orange vest)

....

An awkward teenager

....

Black cats (hey, why not?!)

....

TICKET

UNFORTUNATELY TITLED
REAL BOOKS

Scouting for Boys

· ·

Pooh Gets Stuck

· ·

The Best Dad Is a Good Lover

· ·

Touched: The Jerry Sandusky Story

· ·

*Games You Can Play with Your Pussy and
Lots of Other Stuff Cat Owners Should Know*

· ·

*The Missionary Position: Mother Teresa
in Theory and Practice*

· ·

How to Succeed in Business without a Penis

· ·

The Pocket Book of Boners

....

Images You Should Not Masturbate To

....

Make Your Own Sex Toys

....

Castration: The Advantages and Disadvantages

....

Invisible Dick

....

Scouts in Bondage

....

How People Who Don't Know They're Dead
Attach Themselves to Unsuspecting Bystanders
and What to Do about It

....

How You Can Bowl Better Using Self-Hypnosis

....

You're Sharp Enough to Be Your Own Surgeon

....

Electricity in Gynecology

· ·

The Joy of Uncircumcising!

· ·

The Beginner's Guide to Sex in the Afterlife

· ·

Fancy Coffins to Make Yourself

· ·

Alone in the Woods with Scoutmaster Mike

· ·

Dick, Dick, What Did You Lick?

· ·

Natural Harvest: A Collection of Semen-Based Recipes

· ·

Natural Bust Enlargement with Total Mind Power

· ·

*50 Ways to Use Feminine Hygiene Products
in a Manly Manner (for the Self-Assured Male)*

· ·

PERFECT AUTHORS FOR THE BOOK

These book titles aren't real, but if they were, we know exactly who should write them.

Robots by Anne Droid

Stringed Musical Instruments by Amanda Lynne

Red Vegetables by Bea Troot

The Big Book of Steak by Porter House

Not Optional by Mandy Torry

Six Feet Under by Doug Graves

From Undertaker to Crematorium Operator by Douglas Graves

The Paper Route by Avery Daye

Look Out for That Wall! by Vera Way

My Life as a Pants Salesman by Seymour Butts

Mountain Climbing Techniques by Andover Hand

How Nuclear Weapons Are Made by Adam Baum

....

The Big Blowout by Vlad Tire

....

To Market by Tobias A. Pigg

....

Battle Axes by Tommy Hawk

....

Geography of the Philippines by Archie Pelago

....

Stop Arguing! by Xavier Breath

....

Fun Things to do Outside by Alf Resco

....

Proper Lawn Care by Ray King

....

The Odds of Coin Tossing by Taylor Hedds

....

Installing Carpets by Walter Wahl

....

The Haunted House! by Emma Fraid

....

Championship Tennis Matches by Davis Skupp

....

Housing Construction by Bill Jerome Holmes

....

Why I Hate the Sun by Gladys Knight

....

The Best Book of All Time by Paige Turner

....

TERRIBLE
PRODUCT NAMES

After numerous marketing department meetings, focus groups, test runs, and executive after executive signing off, you'd think that somebody would've noticed that these product names were a bad idea.

Mitsubishi sold the Montero SUV in Spain under the brand name Pajero. In Spanish the word literally means "self-abusing," which Mitsubishi picked because they thought it implied the car was durable and rugged. Except that in Spain, *pajero* has the colloquial meaning of "self-pleasuring."

....

***Gay* used to mean "happy," and the Australian ice cream brand Golden Gaytime still insists that it does. Its four-pack boxes offer "four delicious chances to have a gay time."**

....

Elmer's Glue briefly sold a preloaded caulking gun called the Squeez 'N' Caulk.

....

In 2005, a software company released a touchscreen-enabled dictionary program for the Nintendo DS system called the Touch Dic.

....

One of the most popular insect repellents in Australia is called Wack Off!

....

One of the most popular candy bars
in Belgium is called Big Nuts.

The AIDS crisis hit in the late 1970s and early 1980s,
pretty much ending the existence of an appetite-
suppressant and diet tool called AYDS.

When the movie *Alien vs. Predator* was released, kids
could dress up as the Predator for Halloween with special
monster gloves labeled "Child Predator Hands."

Nads is a very popular hair removal system
manufactured in Australia.

One way to save the rest of a cigarette for later is by
placing it in a small, fireproof plastic container sold
at convenience stores. It's called the Butt Buddy.

A brand of swimming pool chlorinator attempted to combine
the words "Pool" and "Life" and wound up with Poolife.

A popular brand of cola in Ghana: Pee Cola. (Ask for it by name!)

A company called LeCour's sells an off-brand Double
Stuff Oreo knockoff called Double Creme Betweens.

You probably don't want to know about the flavor
notes in a brand of wine called Drysack.

DAD JOKES

Your dad will love these jokes even more
than he loves wearing socks with sandals.

Did you read that new book about beavers?
You should, it's the best dam book to come out this year!

. . . .

Why was the electric car put in jail?
It was charged with battery.

. . . .

Did you hear about the kidnapping in Chicago?
It's okay. He woke up.

. . . .

Did you hear about the rabbit that couldn't find anything to eat?
Not to worry, something is bound to turnip.

. . . .

What do you call a masturbating cow?
Beef Stroganoff.

. . . .

Did you hear about the wheat farmer?
He was outstanding in his field!

. . . .

Telephone operator: I'm sorry about your wait, sir.
Dad: Are you calling me fat?

. . . .

Why wouldn't the lobster donate any money to charity?
It was shellfish.

. . . .

Have you ever been to Prague?
It's really beautiful, you should Czech it out.

HGTV'S
FALL LINEUP

Autumn is just around the corner and that means HGTV has gobs of new shows lined up.

TINY HOUSE EXTREME
Get ready to be wowed! Watch Andrew and the team transform boring tiny houses into extreme tiny houses. Did someone say 3 bedrooms, 2 baths, and full-size galley kitchen? You won't believe how big these tiny houses can be!

DIFFICULT COMPROMISES
Be endlessly entertained by these middle-class house hunters struggling to find decent homes that they can afford. Fantasizing about a walk-in shower with marble tile? Nope, not a chance, Michelle. Always wanted to hang your stockings by the chimney with care? Too bad, Karen, a fireplace is never going to happen! Witness these couples say good-bye to their hopes and dreams as they sign the papers on their brand-new one-bedroom condos.

ARBITRARY REVAMP
Catch all new episodes of fickle homeowners trying their damndest to keep up with the ever-changing landscape of home décor pics on Pinterest. Watch as Farmhouse Industrial expert Erica Mathews cattily exchanges white subway tiles for Carrera white subway tiles. Would you believe some of these people still have stainless appliances? Not to worry; Erica will tell them what's up and swap them for the latest in appliance innovation: black stainless steel.

PROPERTY BROTHERS NIGHTS
Your favorite brothers are back, only this time they're solving crimes. Sexy crimes.

SALVAGERS
We're pretty sure that this is just surveillance footage of meth heads stealing copper wiring from buildings at night. But you're sure to get lots of amazing ideas!

FAIRY HOUSE RENOVATIONS
Are you embarrassed about your subpar backyard fairy house every time you have neighborhood kids over for play dates? Yikes! Not to worry, Makayla and Mackenzie are ready to convert those tree stump disasters into tree stump miracles. Say good-bye to plastic teal doors purchased from Michaels and say hello to wooden magenta doors purchased from Etsy!

OPEN CONCEPT
Walls? Who needs 'em? With a little bit of paint and a whole lot of audacity, tune in to see Kyler and the Krew remove every single wall they come in contact with. That's right, you're essentially watching decent homes being renovated into one giant white room.

BILLBOARDS

THESE ACTUAL BILLBOARDS CERTAINLY MADE AN IMPRESSION.

"Cheap enough to say, 'Phuket I'll go.'"

—Air Asia

....

"Your wife is hot. Time to get your AC fixed."

—an HVAC company

....

"I did WHAT with my sister?"

—Jack Daniel's

....

"Wanted. One nightstand."

—a furniture store

....

"We'd love to be sitting on your face."

—Ray-Ban

....

"Tips. Our waitresses have big TIPS."

—Hooters

....

"We're proud of our privates."

—U.S. Army

....

"Just because you did it doesn't mean you're guilty."

—a lawyer

....

THE BEST WI-FI NETWORK NAMES

Because life's too short to connect to a Linksys network.

House of Horrormones

Wi-Fi Beater

I'm Being Held Captive in a Router

We Can Hear It When You Yell

You're Being Hacked

Password 4 Pizza

CIASurveillance#2251486

Wi-Fis Can't Jump

Sometimes I Use Your Garbage Can

Hail Satan!

It's Good to Have LAN

Searching...

Virus Downloader

Nacho Wi-Fi

Router? I Hardly Knew Her!

Share Your Weed

Password Is Sucker

Bathroomcam3

LAN in the Place Where You Live

Pornhub

Beetlejuice Beetlejuice

My WiiiiiiiFiiiiiii

"Jokes"

These are a variety of humor called "anti-jokes." They're not really jokes, and they're not really funny. Except that they're so not funny and so completely blow up the notion of what a joke is that they're EXTREMELY funny.

What's black, and white, and red all over?
A black, white, and red thing.

....

How do you confuse a blonde woman?
Speak nonsense and then run away.

....

Why was six afraid of seven?
It wasn't. Numbers don't feel fear.

....

Knock-knock.
Who's there?
Your mother.
Oh! Come on in, Mom!

....

"Doctor, doctor, you've got to help me."
"Indeed I do, per the Hippocratic Oath, and because I have chosen to use my medical expertise to treat others."

....

Why did the fireman wear red suspenders?
He couldn't find his yellow ones, which he greatly preferred.

What's red and smells like blue paint?
Red paint.

A man walked into a bar holding a chunk of asphalt under one arm. The bartender said, "What'll it be?" The man said, "A whiskey, and one for the road." The bartender replied, "You mean that chunk of asphalt under your arm?" "Yes, I was just kidding. It's a chunk of asphalt, and so I referred to it as a piece of road, because roads are often made of asphalt." "Oh, I understand," the bartender said. "So just one whiskey, then?" The man answered, "Yes, please."

What did the lawyer say to the other lawyer?
"We are both lawyers."

How many Polish people does it take to change a light bulb?
Just one. It's not hard to change a light bulb.

A horse walked into a bar. Many of the other bar patrons immediately left, as they identified the potential danger in the situation.

What's brown and sticky?
A stick.

Your mother is so fat that she should lose weight
so as to avoid any long-term health risks.

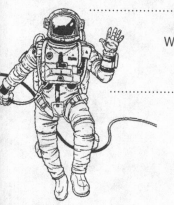

What do you call a woman on the moon?
An astronaut.

What was the last thing the old man
said before he kicked the bucket?
"Hey, how far do you think
I can kick this bucket?"

What's worse than finding a worm in your apple?
Human misery.

What did the farmer say when he lost his tractor?
"I wish I knew where my tractor was."

What's a vampire's favorite fruit?
No matter; vampires are imaginary.

What do you call it when the pope freezes to death?
A terrible tragedy and a leadership crisis
for the Catholic Church.

10

OLD SCHOOL

LITTLE WILLIE
JOKES

They're *not* what you think. These rhymes about a psychotic
little boy named "Willie" (or Willy, Billy, Johnny, Bobby...)
were popular in the late nineteenth century.

Little Willie with a thirst for gore,

Nailed the baby to the door.

Mother said, with humor quaint,

"Willie, dear, don't mar the paint."

. . . .

Willie heard his sister scream,

Went and threw her in the stream.

Said her wails were too absurd.

"Children should be seen, not heard."

. . . .

Willie saw some dynamite,

Couldn't understand it quite.

Curiosity never pays.

It rained Willie seven days.

. . . .

Into the cistern little Willie,
Pushed his little sister, Lillie.
Mother couldn't find her daughter,
So now we sterilize our water.

....

Willie saw a buzz-saw buzz,
Like a bike, and thought it was.
Willie's corpse is full of nicks,
Ain't he cute? He's cut in six!

....

Little Willie, pleasure bent,
Entombed his father in cement.
Mother said, "You little cad,
I think you're rather hard on Dad."

....

Little Willie, temper black,
Tied pa to the railroad track.
Mother said, "You make me sore!
The trains don't run there anymore."

....

Willie looking in the gun,
Pulls the trigger just for fun.
Mother says in accents pained,
"Willie is so scatter-brained!"

Little Willie, always clowning,
Was the cause of papa's drowning.
Mother patted Willie's back.
"Sonny, I look swell in black."

Willie, with the garden shears,
Cut off both the baby's ears.
At the baby, so unsightly,
Mother raised her eyebrows slightly.

Little Willie, with a curse,
Threw the teapot at the nurse.
When it struck her on the nose,
His father cheered, "How straight he throws!"

Baby's in the ice-cream freezer,
Willie turns the crank to squeeze her.
Ma says, "Dear, the way that's fixed,
You'll have the child completely mixed."

Little Willie, full of glee,

Put radium in grandma's tea.

Now he thinks it quite a lark,

To see her shining in the dark.

Willie's cute as cute can be.

Beneath his brother, only three,

He lit a stick of dynamite.

Now brother's simply out of sight.

Willie, I regret to state,

Cut his sister up for bait.

We miss her when it's time to dine,

But Willie's fish taste simply fine.

Willie poisoned his father's tea;

Father died in agony.

Mother came, and looked quite vexed:

"Really, Will," she said, "what next?!"

OLD JOKES

Philogelos, or "Love of Laughter", dates to fourth century Greece. A collection of about 300 jokes, it's the oldest surviving joke book that's ever been found. Here are some highlights that are still pretty funny today (especially because we translated them into English—you're welcome).

A man fell ill, and he promised his doctor that he'd pay him if he recovered. His wife got angry with him for drinking wine while he had a fever. To which he replied, "Do you want me to get healthy and have to pay the doctor?"

A man visited the home of a sick friend, only to be told by the man's wife that the friend had "departed." The man replied, "When he comes back, tell him I stopped by."

A man visited a country estate, and asked if the well water was potable. The owner of the estate told him that it was, and that his own parents once drank from that very well. The visitor replied, "Their necks must have been incredibly long!"

A cheapskate wrote up his will. He named himself his heir.

A jealous landlord saw that his tenants were very happy. So he evicted all of them.

A man had such bad breath that he committed suicide. He wrapped his head up in bandages and asphyxiated on his own breath.

"Doctor, you've got to help me," a man told his doctor. "Whenever I wake up in the morning, I feel dizzy for half an hour." The doctor told him, "Get up half an hour later then."

A man told his doctor that it hurt to lie down, sit down, or stand. The doctor told him, "The only thing left to do is to hang yourself."

"What should we do—eat or have sex?" a newly married man said to his wife. "You can pick either," she replied, "but we're all out of food."

A census-taker went to a home and asked the man who lived there some questions. "If it pleases you, do you have a wife?" "I have a wife," the man replied, "but she does not please me!"

A man who hated his wife attended her funeral. A man walking by asked, "Who is it who rests in peace here?" The man answered, "Now that she's gone, I do!"

Tom Swifties

"These jokes have been around since the 1910s," Tom explained. Okay, so that doesn't exactly work as a Tom Swifty joke, but it is true—these clever, pun-based jokes first got popular more than 100 years ago.

"How 'bout a roll in the hay?" asked Tom loftily.

....

"I got this ballpoint pen from a Yugoslav friend," said Tom acerbically.

....

"Let's not invite any sadists," said Tom demeaningly.

....

"I'm going to get a hair transplant," said Tom baldly.

....

"My wife is going to have a test tube baby," Tom injected artificially.

....

"The executioner has received the tool he needs," said Tom with a heavy accent.

....

"I've got another @#$%*! insect in my pants," said Tom adamantly.

....

"Orgasms are overrated," said Tom anticlimactically.

....

"This is how he murdered the mystery writer," Tom described.

....

"I like measles!" laughed Tom infectiously.

....

"Those bullets can't hurt me," said Tom blankly.

....

"One of the ten finalists in the 'Best Butts' contest
had to drop out," said Tom asininely.

....

"I fixed the toilet," declared Tom, flushed with success.

....

"I've been having an incontinence problem," Tom gushed.

....

"Those ballet students should train naked," said Tom barbarically.

....

"Employees are not allowed to have sex on company property!"
Tom shouted while banging on the table.

....

"These pants are tight!" Tom burst out.

....

"I'm coming!" Tom ejaculated.

....

"I'm dying," Tom croaked.

....

HAR
HAR

MATURE KNOCK-KNOCK JOKES FOR IMMATURE READERS

Come on in, the door's unlocked.
Also, there's no door—this is a book, not a house.

Knock-knock.
Who's there?
Wanda Smellmop.
Wanda Smellmop who?
No thanks, I can smell it from here.

Knock-knock.
Who's there?
Drew Peacock.
Drew Peacock who?
Try Viagra.

. . . .

Knock-knock.
Who's there?
Butch, Jimmy, and Joe.
Butch, Jimmy, and Joe who?
Butch your arms around me, Jimmy a kiss, and let's Joe!

. . . .

Knock-knock.
Who's there?
Ivana.
Ivana who?
Ivana do bad things to you.

. . . .

Knock-knock.
Who's there?
Juicy.
Juicy who?
Juicy that lady that just walked by?

. . . .

Knock-knock.
Who's there?
Budweiser.
Budweiser who?
Budweiser mother taking her clothes off?

. . . .

Knock-knock.
Who's there?
Howie!
Howie who?
Howie gonna hide this dead body?

. . . .

Knock-knock.
Who's there?
Dewey!
Dewey who?
Dewey have to use a condom?

. . . .

Knock-knock.
Who's there?
Khan.
Khan who?
Khan-dom broke, so I hope you're on the pill.

. . . .

Knock-knock.
Who's there?
Tara.
Tara who?
Tara McClosoff now!

. . . .

Knock-knock.
Who's there?
Dozer.
Dozer who?
Dozer da biggest ones I've ever seen!

. . . .

Knock-knock.
Who's there?
Centipede.
Centipede who?
Centipede on the Christmas tree!

. . . .

Knock-knock.
Who's there?
Winner.
Winner who?
My winner's ten inches long.

. . . .

Knock-knock.
Who's there?
Ike.
Ike who?
Ike can rock your world.

. . . .

Knock-knock.
Who's there?
Leslie.
Leslie who?
Leslieve town before
your wife catches us!

. . . .

"LITTLE AUDREY JUST LAUGHED AND LAUGHED..."

These dark and often nonsensical jokes, about a child who sees the bright side in a variety of tragic and horrific situations, were inexplicably popular in the 1930s.

One day Little Audrey and her mother were driving along when suddenly, the car door flew open and Little Audrey's mother fell out. Little Audrey just laughed and laughed, because she knew all the time that her mother had on her light fall suit.

Little Audrey and her younger brother were inspecting a ship. They inspected every inch of it, until the brother decided he wanted to go all the way up into the crow's nest. When he got there, he waved to Little Audrey below, but lost his balance and fell out. Little Audrey looked at the remains of her brother and just laughed and laughed, because she knew her brother could not stand hard ships.

It was very hot one day, and Little Audrey begged her blind grandfather to take her down to the old swimming hole. He did, and Little Audrey dared him to climb up into a tree and dive off into the water, but he was too scared. Little Audrey finally talked him into it, and she just laughed and laughed. She knew all the time that the swimming hole had dried up.

Little Audrey and her grandmother were walking through town when they came upon a crew of men paving the street. They had a steamroller, a cement mixer, and other large machines. Suddenly, the grandmother saw a quarter out on the street and she ran out to get it, but just as she did, the steamroller came along and flattened her. Little Audrey just laughed and laughed, because she knew all the time that it was only a nickel.

Even though her mother warned her not to, Little Audrey was playing with matches one day. After a while, she set her house on fire and it burned to the ground. As they looked at the ashes, the mother said, "Just wait until your father gets home, young lady!" Little Audrey just laughed and laughed. She knew all the time that her father had come home early and had gone to bed to take a nap.

Little Audrey was on a ship, but it capsized and she wound up stranded on a desert island. A tribe of cannibals found her and tied her up while they put on a giant cauldron to boil. Little Audrey just laughed and laughed, because she knew all the time that she was too little to make enough stew to go around.

Little Audrey was walking down the street when a large, scary man jumped out from behind a bush and shouted, "Take off your clothes!" Little Audrey just laughed and laughed, because she knew they wouldn't fit him.

Little Audrey decided to jump out of an airplane. People came from far and wide to witness her jump, and as the plane got high into the air, she saw the crowd that had gathered to watch her parachute down. Little Audrey jumped out of the plane, and she just laughed and laughed, because she didn't have on a parachute.

WALKS INTO A BAR...

Pull up a stool, grab yourself a drink, and laugh at these drunks and their silly drunk jokes.

A priest, a rabbi, and a minister walk into a bar.
The bartender asks, "Hey, is this some kind of a joke?"

....

A bottle of gin walks into a bar. The bartender says,
"Sorry, we don't serve booze here."

....

A grizzled old prospector walks into a bar. The bartender says,
"Sorry, we don't serve miners."

....

London Bridge walks into a bar. The bartender says,
"Sorry, I can't serve you. You're already falling down."

....

A giraffe walks into a bar. He says, "High balls are on me!"

....

A boss walks into a bar. He doesn't do anything and
pats himself on the back for a job well done.

....

A martini walks into a bar. The bartender says,
"Hey, we've got a drink named after you."
The martini replies, "You have a drink named Steve?"

....

A man walks into a bar. He orders a beer, but when he takes out
his wallet to pay he notices he doesn't have any money.

"Hey bartender," he asks. "Any chance you can spot me?"

The bartender replies, "There you are!"

....

The past, the present, and the future walk into a bar.

It was tense.

....

A man walks into a bar. "Ow!" he exclaims,

because the bar was made of metal.

....

A man walks into a barre. He's a terrible ballet dancer.

....

A horse walks into a bar. The bartender says,

"Hey, why the long face?"

....

A man walks into a barn. A horse says,

"Hey, why the long face?"

....

A teetotaler walks into a bar. The bartender says,

"Hey, why the wrong place?"

....

A dyslexic man walks into a bra.

....

PIRATE JOKES

Ye be warned: these jokes be arrrrrgh-rated.

What do horny pirates hate?
A sunken chest with no booty.

....

Pirates are usually excellent singers.
They love to hit the high-Cs.

....

What does a pirate eat for breakfast?
C-c-c-c-c-c-ereal.

....

What has no arms, no legs, no eyes, and a parrot?
The world's greatest pirate!

....

Why did the pirate take his favorite wench ashore?

She said she wanted to see his dock.

Why are pirates difficult to be in a relationship with?

They only like to hook-up.

What did the pirate nickname his leg?

Peg.

What did the pirate say after he went blind in battle?

"Eye-eye!"

What did the pirate find in the ship's toilet?

The captain's log.

Where did the captain keep his buccaneers?

On the sides of his buccan' head.

How does a lonely pirate spend the evening?

He mastARRRRbates.

When you're a pirate, every call
is a booty call.

HUMAN BEHAVIOR

A VERY TERRIBLE GAME OF
"WOULD YOU RATHER?"

The choice is yours, so choose wisely, my friend.

Stick your thumb up your grandpa's butt,
or not have a mobile phone for a year?

Kill a majestic white owl with your bare hands,
or live on mayonnaise sandwiches for
the rest of your life?

Not be able to wash your clothing for one year,
or let R. Kelly pee on you for an entire evening?

Have near-constant life-hindering diarrhea, or tell every new person you meet that you're a Nazi?

· ·

Have spinal herpes, or change your legal name
to Pumpkin Spice Latte?

· ·

**Be the proud owner of the world's longest
toenails, or bathe in a portable toilet?**

WC

· ·

Marry a hippie, or a bowl of minestrone?

· ·

**Take a seven-week taxidermy course,
or become a part-time snail farmer?**

· ·

Play a *Monopoly* game that might not
ever end, or exercise?

· ·

IDIOMS FROM AROUND THE WORLD THAT JUST DON'T TRANSLATE

An idiom is an absurd, well-known phrase with a commonly understood meaning—like how in English, "it's raining cats and dogs" means "it's raining very hard." A non-English speaker might be completely flummoxed by that, as might you be by these real expressions from other languages.

Armenian: "Glukhs mi ardukeer!"
Translation: "Stop ironing my head!"
Meaning: "Stop bugging me!"

....

Cheyenne: "Mónésó'táhoenôtse kosa?"
Translation: "Are you still riding the goat?"
Meaning: "Are you still married?"

....

Czech: "Chodit kolem horké kaše"
Translation: "I won't walk around in hot porridge."
Meaning: It's like saying "I won't beat around the bush."

....

French: "J'ai d'autres chats à fouetter!"
Translation: "I have other cats to whip!"
Meaning: "I've got other fish to fry!"

....

German: "Leben wie die made im speck!"
Translation: "I'm living like a maggot in bacon!"
Meaning: A person is living a life of luxury.

....

French: "Pédaler dans le choucroute."
Translation: "Pedaling through sauerkraut."
Meaning: Getting nowhere.

....

Polish: "Wypchad sid sianem!"
Translation: "Get stuffed with hay!"
Meaning: "Go f*** yourself!"

....

Portuguese: "A vaca foi pro brejo"
Translation: "The cow went to the swamp."
Meaning: "This is hopeless."

....

Portuguese: "Fazer boca de siri."
Translation: "To make a crab's mouth."
Meaning: To be secretive or discreet.

....

Portuguese: "Lavar a égua."
Translation: To wash a female horse.
Meaning: To win a lot of money at gambling.

....

Irish Gaelic: "Aithníonn ciaróg ciaróg eile."
Translation: "Beetles recognize each other."
Meaning: "It takes one to know one."

....

Dutch: "Ik zal ze een poepie laten ruiken!"
Translation: "I shall let them smell a poppy!"
Meaning: "Oh yeah? Well, I'll show them!"

....

German: "Tomaten auf den augen haben."
Translation: "You've got tomatoes on your eyes."
Meaning: "You've got blinders on."

....

German: "Die katze im sack kaufen."
Translation: "Buy a cat in a sack."
Meaning: To buy something sight unseen.

....

Swedish: "Det är ingen ko på isen."
Translation: "There's no cow on the ice."
Meaning: "Don't worry."

....

Swedish: "Att glida in på en räkmacka."
Translation: "Slide in on a shrimp sandwich."
Meaning: A person who has coasted through life thanks to money or family connections.

....

Russian: "Muda labudova!"
Translation: "The balls of a swan!"
Meaning: "It's impossible!"

....

Spanish: "Me costó un riñón."
Translation: "It cost me a kidney."
Meaning: "It cost me an arm and a leg."

....

Email Subject Translations

HERE'S A HANDY GUIDE THAT YOU CAN USE
TO DECIPHER WHAT'S GOING TO BE IN
AN EMAIL WITHOUT EVEN HAVING TO OPEN IT!

"Quick question" = I have 12 questions, four of which you shouldn't and won't have any clue about.

....

No subject line = I am an enigma wrapped inside a beautiful mystery that will take you hours, nay *days*, to unravel.

....

"Re: Your Project" = I was hoping I could trick you into thinking this was a response to an email you had previously written me and therefore get your attention.

....

"Uh oh! You forgot to update your time card!" = I have difficulty expressing my authority over you so I will talk like a three-year-old to make us both feel more comfortable.

....

"As You Wish" = This is guaranteed to be from your office IT guy. But cut him a break, he doesn't have a clue that nearly everything he says is creepy.

....

"Urgent" = Not even remotely urgent.

....

"OCTOBER INVOICE" = The sender is obviously emailing you from a busy nightclub. Or perhaps they're hang-gliding. Either way, by the looks of the caps-lock, shouting is absolutely necessary.

....

"Hi" = Who knows? This subject line might even be more mysterious than no subject line at all.

....

FWD: FWD: FWD: FWD: FWD: FWD: FWD: FWD: FWD: = Do not open under any circumstances.

....

UGLY JOKES

U.G.L.Y. These jokes ain't got no alibi. They **UGLY.**

A woman got onto the bus with her very ugly baby. The driver said, "Lady, that's the ugliest baby I've ever seen." "Why, I never!" the woman shouted before taking a seat in the back of the bus. A man sitting nearby asked, "Hey lady, what's wrong?" "That bus driver insulted me!" the woman cried. "Well, don't you take that from him," the man said. "You go back up there and tell him off!" "You know what?" the woman said. "I think I will!" "Great!" the man said. "Here, let me hold your monkey."

Did you hear about the world's ugliest man? When he tried to take a selfie his phone pretended that it didn't have enough space.

You know you're ugly when everybody wants
to take a group picture and you're the one
who takes the picture.

There was this guy who was so ugly
that when he looked in the mirror, the
mirror went on its lunch break.

There was this one kid who was so ugly that
when his mom dropped him off at school in the
morning, a cop gave her a ticket for littering.

Did you hear about the world's ugliest chef?
Whenever he cut onions, the onions cried.

Did you hear about the world's ugliest farmer?
He didn't need a scarecrow because every time
he went outside the crows flew away.

Did you hear about the
ugliest man in Australia?
He threw a boomerang
and it didn't come back.

....

Where can you find pictures
of the world's ugliest baby?
Oh, your mom's still
probably got a few.

....

Late one Friday night, a man heads to the checkout
of a grocery store and places his items on the
conveyor belt. The cashier sees the individual frozen
pizza, a single soda, and the *Sports Illustrated*
swimsuit issue. "So," she says. "Single, huh?" The
man looks down at his purchases, knowingly
chuckles, and says, "How could you tell?" The
cashier replies, "Because you're so incredibly ugly."

....

RIPPED FROM THE
HEADLINES

These tabloid headlines may be real, but the stories that accompanied them probably aren't.

ASTEROID TO BOUNCE OFF EARTH TODAY

....

NASA TAKES PHOTO OF GHOSTS IN SPACE

....

GHOST KICKED OUT OF CEMETERY

....

DOLPHIN GROWS HUMAN ARMS

....

ABE LINCOLN WAS A WOMAN

....

CHAOS CLOUD TAKES VIRGINIA

....

JOHN GOTTI'S GHOST IS RUNNING MAFIA

....

FAT CAT OWNS 23 OLD LADIES

....

MAN GIVES BIRTH TO A HEALTHY BABY BOY

....

SECOND POPE UNDER POPE HAT! SCANDAL! MORE POPES TO COME?

....

COOKIE MONSTER MUGS KIDS IN TIMES SQUARE

....

LOCH NESS MONSTER FOUND DEAD

....

CROCODILE DUNDEE FOUND ALIVE!

....

SEVERED LEG HOPS TO HOSPITAL!

....

HORSE BORN WITH HUMAN FACE

....

JERSEY DEVIL SPOTTED IN OKLAHOMA

....

OOMPA LOOMPA SHOWED ME HIS WILLY WONKA

....

GIANT'S ARM FALLS ON CAR

....

DONKEY ROBS BANK

....

WILD HOGS TAKE ATLANTA!

....

WORLD'S UGLIEST WOMAN DIED AS SHE TOOK LOOK IN MIRROR

....

SATURN IS A GIANT UFO!

....

ABBRVTNS PLZ

As a culture, we're using more and more abbreviations in our online interactions and IRL conversations. Does this mean we're getting smarter or dumber? Lazier or more efficient?

GOAT. LL Cool J has been calling himself "The GOAT" for years. No, he doesn't live in a meadow and eat tin cans—it stands for "greatest of all time," and he means that he's the greatest of all time at rapping.

. . . .

Stan. Before you can make fun of obsessive fans of a particular celebrity or TV show, they make fun of themselves with the suffix "-stan." It's a contraction of "STalker" and "fAN," as in "Randy is a total Bananaramastan."

. . . .

Ship. When stans of a TV show get online and talk about how they want two characters to hook up, they are "shipping," or hoping that a relation*ship* forms.

. . . .

IDK. It takes the same number of syllables to say "IDK" as it does to say "I don't know," but it's a heck of a lot quicker to type.

. . . .

SMH. When you are frustrated with another's behavior, you might tell them they made you "shake [my] head."

. . . .

Hunty. This word originated in the drag queen community, but made its way into the rest of society because drag queens are clever and hilarious. It's a combination of "honey" and a certain unspeakable C-word, except that it's used in a positive way instead of an insult. Hunty means, essentially, "awesome" or "fierce."

. . . .

V. It means "very." (Unless you're an ancient Roman, in which case it means "five.")

. . . .

JOMO. "FOMO" is out; "JOMO" is in. The former stands for "fear of missing out," or seeing all of your friends on social media having fun while you're stuck at home. The latter is quite the opposite—it means the "joy of missing out," that special feeling when one sees all their friends doing something on social media that looks regrettable and horrible, like waiting in line for three hours for brunch, or going to a concert.

. . . .

Trill. It's a contraction and subsequent re-spelling of the words "true" and "real." It comes from the world of hip-hop and is used as a term of respect.

. . . .

SUS. Someone who is shady and not to be trusted, as it stands for suspect and/or suspicious.

. . . .

Suh. This one is an argument for the "abbreviations are making us dumber" contingent. It's a shortening of "sup," which itself is a shortening of "wassup," which *itself* is short for "what's up?" It's a suh-ception!

. . . .

BANNED
Baby Names

Many countries have naming laws. That means if you live there, you can't name your baby certain things—like offensive or embarrassing names—or you have to choose from a pre-approved list. Here are some attempted but rejected names from around the world.

Anal (New Zealand)

....

Fish and Chips (New Zealand)

....

Keenan Got Lucky (New Zealand)

....

Cinderella Beauty Blossom (New Zealand)

....

Talula Does the Hula from Hawaii (New Zealand)

....

Fat Boy (New Zealand)

....

Monkey (Denmark)

....

Superman (Sweden)

Metallica (Sweden)

Brfxxccxxmnpcccclllmmnprxvclmnckssqlbb11116 (Sweden)

Smelly Head (Malaysia)

007 (Malaysia)

Nutella (France)

Mini Cooper (France)

Osama Bin Laden (Germany)

Stompie (Germany)

Enrique (Iceland)

Rambo (Mexico)

Batman (Mexico)

....

Robocop (Mexico)

....

Circumcision (Mexico)

....

Rihanna (Portugal)

....

Viking (Portugal)

....

Elvis (Sweden)

....

Friday (Italy)

....

Devil (Japan)

....

@ (China)

....

Grammophon (Germany)

....

Albuquerque (Portugal)

....

WEIRD PRODUCTS

THERE ARE SOME THINGS PEOPLE NEED (SHELTER, CLOTHING), AND THERE ARE SOME THINGS PEOPLE WANT (NETFLIX, KEY CHAINS THAT MAKE FART NOISES). THEN THERE'S STUFF LIKE THIS, WHICH DOESN'T QUITE FALL INTO EITHER CATEGORY.

FREEDOM FLASK. Have you ever relieved yourself at a urinal and wished that your organ delivered something useful instead of all that dumb urine, like, say, beer? Of course you have; everybody has done that. Make your dream a reality with this flask that hides in the pants, then feed the tube through your fly, and impress your friends with your new "ability."

· · · · · · · ·

WAVE BOX. Say you're in the car and have a hankering for popcorn, or you've got a frozen pizza and the kitchen is, like, 20 whole feet away. Get yourself a Wave Box. It's a portable microwave oven!

. . . .

HOG WILD TWIRLING SPAGHETTI FORK. So you're eating a big bowl of pasta and you want to swirl up a whole bunch on your fork, but what if you don't have a spoon to use for leverage, or the energy or know-how to do it at all? Problem solved with this battery-operated, self-propelled twirling fork.

. . . .

EXTRA MANLY BACON-SCENTED FAKE MUSTACHE. There are, of course, hundreds of fine, high-quality fake mustaches on the market today. But only one smells like imitation bacon. (It's this one.)

. . . .

SOCK BUDDY. Sick and tired of fumbling around with your socks for 15 seconds each morning? Sock Buddy makes it easier to put on your socks. Just slip your sock in Sock Buddy, put it by your feet, and Sock Buddy will take it from there.

· · · · · · · · ·

BOB ROSS CHIA PET. One of the many varieties available of the Chia Pet ("ch-ch-ch-chia!") is this one made in the image of the "happy little trees"–loving PBS painter.

· · · · · · · · ·

ASIAN OLD MAN PEEL-AND-STICK WALL DECAL. Well, that's pretty much what it is. Just peel and stick this life-size decal of an elderly Asian man over your bed, in the kitchen, or anywhere else you please.

· · · · · · · · ·

DOGBRELLA: THE UMBRELLA FOR DOGS. Don't want your puppy getting wet? Just get them their own umbrella (it stays fixed above their head when attached to a leash) and you'll never smell wet dog again.

· · · · · · · · ·

LOFTUS LIPS DICK. When was the last time there was a true innovation in lipstick? The future is now with this compact cosmetic. Available in many lovely shades, the tube looks exactly like a penis. The other girls will be *so* jealous when they see you doing your after-lunch touch-ups.

· · · · · · · · ·

BOYFRIEND PILLOW COMPANION. When hubby's out on a "business trip," this adult man-shaped pillow is there for you. Just snuggle up with it like you wish your man would, and let your spirits rise.

· · · · · · · · ·

12

THE
FINAL
CHAPTER

WHAT'S THE DIFFERENCE?!

What's the difference between these jokes and other jokes in the book? These jokes are in the "what's the difference..." format. (And that's no joke.)

What's the difference between a stamp and a woman?

One's a mail fee, and the other's a female.

....

What's the difference between a fisherman and a "D" student?

One baits hooks, and the other hates books.

....

What's the difference between a hippo and a Zippo?

One's very heavy, but the other is a little lighter.

....

**What's the difference between a churchgoer
and a person taking a bath?**

One has hope in their soul, and the
other has soap in their hole.

....

What's the difference between a newborn and a really old man?

Depends.

....

What's the difference between a snowman and a snow-woman?

Snowballs.

....

**What's the difference between a run-over skunk
and a run-over lawyer?**

The vultures aren't gagging at the skunk.

....

What's the difference between a carp and a lawyer?

One is a scum-sucking bottom-feeder, and the other is a fish.

....

**What's the difference between Mick Jagger
and a Scottish sheep farmer?**

One says, "Hey, you, get off of my cloud,"
and the other says, "Hey, McCloud, get off of my sheep!"

....

What's the difference between boogers and vegetables?

Kids won't eat vegetables.

....

**What's the difference between a corn husker with epilepsy
and a prostitute with irritable bowel syndrome?**

One shucks between fits and the other...

What's the difference between an Irish wedding and an Irish funeral?

The funeral has one less drunk person.

What's the difference between a pregnant woman and a light bulb?

The light bulb can be unscrewed.

**What's the difference between fresh roadkill
and a dead trombone player?**

The dead animal was on its way to a gig.

What's the difference between goldfish and hillbillies?

Goldfish muck about fountains, and hillbillies...

What's the difference between an onion and the bagpipes?

No one ever cries when you cut up a set of bagpipes.

What's the difference between a dapper man riding
a unicycle and a slob riding a bicycle?

Attire.

What's the difference between Dubai and Abu Dhabi?

The people in Dubai don't watch *The Flintstones*,
but the people in Abu Dhabi do.

What's the difference between
Santa Claus and a dog?

Santa wears a suit, while a dog just pants.

What's the difference between an old bus stop
and a crab with breast implants?

One's a crusty bus station, and the other
is a busty crustacean.

What's the difference between
toilet paper and a shower curtain?

Wait, so... you don't know?

VERY BAD
Website Addresses

When establishing your home on the Internet, please remember that a website's address doesn't have spaces, and when you combine words, it creates new words. Disgusting, filthy, hilarious words.

Pen Island, a seller of writing instruments online at...

Penisland.com

A talent agency directory called Who Represents can be found at...

Whorepresents.com

Therapist Finder locates therapists. Only therapists. Its address is...

therapistfinder.com

Despite the URL, design firm Speed of Art has nothing to do with Speedos or flatulence:

Speedofart.com

This is the address of an information technology salvaging service, or "IT scrapping," so they have the URL...

itscrap.com

You can find financial planner Benjamin Dover at

bendover.con

....

Learn more about New York's many waterways at

nycanal.com

....

Mole Station Native Nursery is a plant nursery in Australia.
See what's blooming at...

molestationnursery.com

....

Single? Over 40? Live near Boston? Jewish? You may want to check out
North of Boston Jewish Singles... or maybe not, because its URL is...

nobjs.org

....

Nobody named Emma works at **Analemma.org**. It's a site run
by the Analemma Society, an astronomical organization that
named itself after an astronomical term.

....

La Drape International sells bedspreads and other
fabric-based items in the U.K. Its website:

Ladrape.co.uk

....

YO MAMA HAS EARNED OUR RESPECT!

Because all of our mothers are delightful women who gave birth to us and raised us, here are some extremely polite "yo mama" jokes.

Yo mama has perfectly balanced the demands of her career with her duties as a mother, and has excelled at both!

....

Yo mama is so smart, she studied physics at an Ivy League college and later won a Nobel Prize for her groundbreaking discoveries regarding the nature of subatomic particles!

....

Yo mama is so charitable she gave away a lot of her clothes to the Goodwill, and also washed and folded them first!

....

Yo mama's future is so bright, she's gotta wear shades! She also wants to protect her eyes from the sun's harmful UV rays, because that is important!

....

Yo mama's so kind, she donated her kidney to a dying child she'd never even met!

....

Yo mama's so rich that she set up a college fund for that same child!

....

Yo mama is so smart that she started your college fund the day you were born, and a 401K for you the day you graduated high school!

....

Yo mama's so adorable that cats email each other pictures of her!

....

Yo mama's so supportive that she likes all your Instagram photos just a few seconds after you post them!

....

Yo mama's so chill that you feel like you can discuss personal issues with her in an environment completely free of judgment!

Yo mama is so nice that she always tips 25 percent, regardless of the quality of service!

Yo mama is so fit because she wants to live a long, healthy life and enjoy her grandchildren, if and when you decide to have them!

Yo mama is so sweet that she bought ME a birthday gift. I'm not even her child!

Yo mama looks so youthful that when someone asks if she's your sister, it's in earnest!

Yo mama is so festive that she completely and creatively decorates her house for each and every holiday, both major and minor!

Yo mama is so thoughtful that she always has plenty of food to offer unexpected guests!

....

Yo mama is so industrious that you'd be lucky to inherit even a scrap of her work ethic!

....

Yo mama is so fashionable, she can even rock that neon blue fanny pack you bought her for Mother's Day when you were 10.

....

Yo mama is so pretty that when she went to a fashion show, they put a dress on her and asked her to walk the runway.

....

Yo mama is so awesome that if you look up "awesome" in the dictionary, there's just a picture there of yo mama.

....

HILARIOUS IRISH SAYINGS ·

No other culture has a way with words quite like the Irish. Here are a few sayings that are best shared after you and your mates have had a few too many.

A turkey never voted for an early Christmas.

Do not mistake a goat's beard for a fine stallion's tail.

Even a tin knocker will shine on a dirty door.

It's difficult to choose between two blind goats.

A silent mouth is sweet to hear.

Show the fatted calf but not the thing that fattened him.

If you put a silk dress on a goat, he is still a goat.

You've got to do your own growing,
no matter how tall your grandfather was.

**As you slide down the bannister of life, may the
splinters never point the wrong direction.**

May your life be filled with so much
laughter that the tears run down your leg.

**Never approach a bull from the front, a horse
from the rear, or an idiot from any direction.**

He who laughs last, thinks slowest.

There's nothing so bad it couldn't be worse.

SNAPPY COMEBACKS

You know how when somebody says something mean or dumb to you and you think of the perfect comeback... an hour later when you're driving home? These amazing folks thought of the best possible send-up in the moment!

Woman: Mr. Coolidge, I've made a bet against a fellow who said it was impossible to get more than two words out of you.
President Calvin Coolidge: You lose.

. . . .

George Bernard Shaw sent a note to English prime minister Winston Churchill inviting him to the opening night of a play. "Have reserved two tickets for opening night. Come and bring a friend if you have one."
Churchill wrote back, "Impossible to come to first night. Will come to second night, if you have one."

. . . .

Lady Astor: Winston, if you were my husband, I'd put poison in your coffee.
Winston Churchill: Nancy, if you were my wife, I'd drink it.

. . . .

Noel Coward remarked on writer Edna Ferber wearing a suit. "You look almost like a man," Coward quipped. Ferber replied, "So do you."

. . . .

Responding to a rumor that President Richard Nixon had called him an asshole, Canadian prime minister Pierre Trudeau remarked, "I've been called worse things by better men."

. . . .

Pope John Paul XXIII was once asked by a reporter, "How many people work in the Vatican?" "About half," he answered.

. . . .

Truman Capote once signed an autograph for a woman. For some reason, her drunk husband wasn't happy about that, went up to the writer, and took his penis out of his pants. He told Capote to "put your signature on that." Capote looked down and said, "I don't know about my signature, but I can initial it."

. . . .

After a screening of *The Brown Bunny* at the 2003 Cannes Film Festival, critic Roger Ebert said the movie was the worst film to ever screen at the annual event. *Brown Bunny* director Vincent Gallo responded by labeling Ebert a "fat pig with the physique of a slave trader." Ebert's retort: "It is true that I am fat, but one day I will be thin, and he will still be the director of *The Brown Bunny*."

. . . .

YOU'RE NOT HELPING,
AUTOCORRECT

Whilst jamming your thumbs into your phone screen's tiny keyboard, it's easy to hit the wrong letter, triggering the autocorrect function to change the word to what it "thinks" you meant. It's usually right, but when it's wrong . . . it's **very** wrong.

Tried to type: "Correction"
Autocorrected to: "Erection"
As used in a text: "No, I can't go out, my boss needs to do a bunch of erections."

....

Tried to type: "Pencil"
Autocorrected to: "Penis"
As used in a text: "Do you have a penis I can borrow?"

....

Tried to type: "Santa"
Autocorrected to: "Satan"
As used in a text: "Only 4 more days until Satan comes!"

....

Tried to type: "Fifty"
Autocorrected to: "Titty"
As used in a text: "You still owe me titty from last weekend."

....

Tried to type: "Aunt"
Autocorrected to: "Cunt"
As used in a text: "Hi sweetie, sorry to tell you but your cunt died."

....

Tried to type: "Hungry"
Autocorrected to: "Horny"
As used in a text: "I'm so horny I haven't had anything all day."

....

Tried to type: "Meditating"
Autocorrected to: "Masturbating"
As used in a text: "Sorry I didn't hear your text, I was masturbating."

....

Tried to type: "Coke"
Autocorrected to: "Cock"
As used in a text: "Pick me up a cock on your way home?"

....

Tried to type: "Drink"
Autocorrected to: "Dicks"
As used in a text: "Wanna go out for dicks tonight?"

....

Tried to type: "Epi pen"
Autocorrected to: "Epic penis"
As used in a text: "Don't forget to pack your epic penis!"

....

Tried to type: "Vanilla"
Autocorrected to: "Vaginal"
As used in a text: "They were out of chocolate so I got you vaginal."

....

Tried to type: "Volvo"
Autocorrected to: "Vulva"
As used in a text: "Those new hybrid Vulvas are beautiful!"

....

Tried to type: "Linkin Park"
Autocorrected to: "Kinky fuck"
As used in a text: "Did you watch that kinky fuck video I sent you?"

....

Tried to type: "Mistletoe"
Autocorrected to: "Camel toe"
As used in a text: "I wouldn't mind getting caught under the camel toe with you."

....

Tried to type: "Caps lock"
Autocorrected to: "Cock slap"
As used in a text: "Turn off your cock slap!"

....

Tried to type: "Pumas"
Autocorrected to: "Penis"
As used in a text: "Where'd you get those fresh penis you were wearing today, bro?"

....

Tried to type: "Kissed"
Autocorrected to: "Killed"
As used in a text: "And then he walked me to my door and killed me!"

....

Tried to type: "Dimples"
Autocorrected to: "Nipples"
As used in a text: "Nothing cuter than a girl with nipples."

....

Tried to type: "Fizz"
Autocorrected to: "Jizz"
As used in a text: "Get champagne instead of wine. I want something with some jizz."

....

Tried to type: "Gum"
Autocorrected to: "Cum"
As used in a text: "I've got cum in my hair!"

....

THE PERFECT NAME FOR THE JOB

HELLO
MY NAME IS

What follows are a bunch of examples of **APTRONYMS**, a type of word in which a person's name matches up exactly with their occupation or claim to fame. It's like they were born to do what they do!

One of the fastest runners ever is Olympic gold medalist... Usain BOLT.

....

There are few poets regarded more highly than the nineteenth-century Romantic... William WORDSWORTH.

....

From 1981 to 1987, President Reagan's White House spokesman was a man named... Larry SPEAKES.

....

In 2017, a former congressman was sent to prison for texting picture of his genitals to a minor. That man's name is... Anthony WEINER.

That TV infomercial guy who aggressively shills merchandise like the ShamWow is named... Vince OFFER.

One of the best tennis players to ever hit the court was named... Margaret COURT.

You can bet that this world champion poker player is going to win big. His name is... Chris MONEYMAKER.

Okay, so it's pronounced "bass" not "base," but still, it's pretty great that the guy who sang the bass parts for the boy band NSYNC is named... Lance BASS.

This San Antonio Spurs legend was over seven feet tall, and so he dunked a lot. His name is... Tim DUNCAN.

From 1986 to 1991, this NFL quarterback chucked the ball long distances. That guy is... Chuck LONG.

Secretary of Education under George W. Bush was an educator named... Margaret SPELLINGS.

What's the name of the guy who has produced rock albums for Joan Jett, Bon Jovi, Metallica, and Motley Crue, among other rock bands? A guy named... Bob ROCK.

"Alto" is a type of saxophone, which is played with the use of wooden reeds. The longtime alto sax player for Bob Seger's Silver Bullet Band is musician... Alto REED.

A dominant researcher in clinical psychiatry focusing on anxiety is German researcher... Jules ANGST.

Twice in his 25-year career, this pitcher led his team to a win on the opening day of the season. Who got those early wins? Hall of Famer... Early WYNN.

Judge not lest ye be judged. But the chief justice of England's highest court was named... Igor JUDGE.

A BUCKET LIST
FOR THE BORING

Because not everybody can run a marathon,
go to Paris, or swim with the dolphins.

Get the **Costco** executive membership.

Try a soft taco.

Pet a dog.

Ride in a minivan.

Wear an ironed shirt.

Sign up for Hulu.

Take a nap in the middle of the day.

Fill in a fro-yo punch-card and get that ninth fro-yo for free.

Finish cleaning out the garage.

Wear sunglasses.

Take a selfie.

Eat breakfast for dinner.

Watch a friend skydive.

Put together a really hard puzzle.

Stay up until midnight.

FUNNY
LAST WORDS

We'd all like to go out on a profound note.
Barring that, it's pretty awesome when
the final thing that comes out of
your mouth is clever and witty.

HA-HA!

Jack Soo was a character actor best known for playing
Detective Yemana on *Barney Miller.* There was a running gag
on the police precinct sitcom that Yemana made terrible
coffee. Soo died of cancer in 1979, in the middle of the show's
run. An operation to save his life proved unsuccessful, but just
before he went under the knife, he said to friends and family,
"It must have been the coffee."

Brendan Behan is one of the finest authors to ever come out of Ireland. He died in 1964 in the care of the nun-nurses in a hospital operated by the Catholic Church. His last words were to one of those nurses: "Bless you, sister. May all your sons be bishops."

· · · · · · · · · · · · · · · · · · · ·

Princess Marie-Louise Thérèse was a member of the House of Savoy, a family that once held claim to the French crown. As she lay dying in 1799, she farted. While that would have been a fine final utterance, she then added, "Good. A woman who can fart is not dead." (Then, of course, she died.)

· · · · · · · · · · · · · · · · · · · ·

Nostradamus was always predicting stuff—that was sort of his "thing," writing huge books of chilling prophecy about world events in the centuries to come. His final words were also prophetic, but on a smaller scale. His last night on earth, he reportedly quipped, "Tomorrow, at sunrise, I shall no longer be here." He died overnight.

· · · · · · · · · · · · · · · · · · · ·

Terry Kath was an original member of the band Chicago, back in the '60s and '70s. In 1978, he was at a party and thought it would be fun to play around with a handgun. That made other partygoers nervous, but Kath reassured them by saying, "What do you think I'm gonna do? Blow my brains out?" Then Kath (accidentally) blew his brains out.

· · · · · · · · · · · · · · · · · · · ·

The legendarily crabby drummer **Buddy Rich** died after a 1987 operation. Before he went under, a nurse tried to ask him about drug allergies and asked, "Is there anything you can't take?" Rich said, "Yeah, country music."

. . . .

Author **Richard Feynman** died in 1988 after an illness. His last words: "This dying is boring."

. . . .

James W. Rodgers was convicted of murder in 1957 and sentenced to death by firing squad. At the time of the execution in 1960, he was asked the customary, "Any last requests?" Rodgers said, "Bring me a bulletproof vest." (Request denied.)

. . . .

Actor **W. C. Fields** had a caustic wit up until the moment of his death in 1946. Speaking to Carlotta Monti, his mistress of many years, Fields said, "G** d*** the whole friggin' world and everyone in it but you, Carlotta."

. . . .

Australian composer **Percy Grainger** echoed that sentiment in 1961. His last words were to his wife, Ella: "You're the only one I like."

. . . .

About the Author

KATIE ADAMS is a writer and contributor to over 30 best-selling trivia, nonfiction, and humor books. She also fills the insatiable void of the Internet with endless hours of entertaining content. In her free time, Katie enjoys practicing her epigrammatic wit on her tolerant and loving family in the Pacific Northwest.